Sex is a minefield, and never more so than in adolescence. Yet in her work on sex education, Carol Lee finds that, be it doctors, parents or politicians, the typical attitude is the 'ostrich position' and this, she argues, is dangerous for us all.

In this challenging book, the author traces what has made us adopt the ostrich position. She describes a society not so much permissive as dismissive — at least of young people. She re-defines the image we have of teenagers, showing how ignorance and unhappiness often underlies surface bravado.

With warmth and humour, this book explains the fears we adults have about our own and our children's sexuality. Prejudice and lack of under-standing are all around us. For the sake of the next and future generations we must remove our heads from the sand.

Carol Lee is a journalist and a writer. She has also, for the past ten years, taught sex education in Britain and has lectured in America and Canada.

THE OSTRICH POSITION

POSITION

Sex, schooling and mystification

CAROL LEE

London
UNWIN PAPERBACKS
Boston   Sydney

This edition first published in Great Britain by Writers and Readers
Cooperative Society Ltd. 1983
First published by Unwin Paperbacks 1986

UNWIN ® PAPERBACKS
40 Museum Street, London WC1A 1LU, UK

Unwin Paperbacks
Park Lane, Hemel Hempstead, Herts HP2 4TE, UK

Allen & Unwin Australia Pty Ltd
8 Napier Street, North Sydney, NSW 2060, Australia

Unwin Paperbacks with the Port Nicholson Press
PO Box 11−838 Wellington, New Zealand

Copyright © Carol Lee, 1983, 1986

ISBN 0 04 613065 9

British Library Cataloguing in Publication Data

Lee, Carol
    The ostrich position: sex, schooling and
    mystification.
1.   Youth—Sexual behavior
I.   Title
306.7'088055   HQ27
ISBN 0−04−613065−9

Printed in Great Britain by
Hazell Watson and Viney Ltd, Member of the BPCC, Aylesbury, Bucks

Contents

Dedication

To the pupils,
with my thanks for their kindness and affection.

Acknowledgements

I would like to thank Foster Walker, University of Alberta, Edmonton, without whom this book would not have been possible. I would also like to thank Peter Martin, Anthony Rudolf, Francesca Greenoak and the teachers who have helped and supported this work.

Preface

The Family Planning Association welcomes this book as a valuable resource for parents, teachers and other professionals. Carol Lee was trained by the FPA as a sex educator at the time when the association still sent speakers into schools to assist them in their task of education in personal relationships and sexuality. The views in this book are not necessarily those of the FPA but are based on Carol's work in schools, and will provide inspiration and insight to others working in the field.

As Carol makes clear, both she and the FPA strongly believe that sex education must not only give information and increase understanding, it must also promote responsible behaviour, combat exploitation, cultivate the ability to make informed decisions, and develop educational skills for future parents and child carers. Its fundamental philosophy is profoundly moral in that it values individuals and enables them to value other people. Carol talks of 'giving young people a sense of their own dignity, of their own wholesomeness'.

It is sometimes argued that only parents should have a responsibility for young people's sex education, but 'what would happen to the children of parents who did not have the time or skills to educate at home?' With the current greater awareness of child sexual abuse (most of which occurs within the family) it is even more crucial that there are alternative and sensitive sources of information, advice and help for children who might be at risk.

This book is not intended to be a 'textbook' nor a guide to what should be done. What is taught in any particular school or class will depend on many factors including the school policy, the skills and qualities of the teachers, the emotional and intellectual development of the young people, and their religious and ethnic backgrounds. Since 1980 the FPA has concentrated on offering a training and consultancy service to teachers to enable them to deal with relationships and sexual issues within their own work, and it is no longer FPA policy or practice to send visiting speakers into schools.

The FPA would support and echo Carol Lee's final plea:

At the moment fulfilling relationships are lost to thousands of young people through lack of example and through their failure to express themselves. Rather than shying away from our responsibilities to educate as fully as possible — to educate for life and living — I think we should be moving firmly and rapidly towards them.'

The Family Planning Association

1 Sex by Any Other Name

WHEN TALKING about sex with teenagers there is one major problem — language. English may be rich if you want to talk about anything else, but if sex is your subject there is little to speak of — or with. It is not surprising therefore that young people have made up their own language to describe sex, an alternative vocabulary which we, for the most part, find distasteful. In their terms you do not 'masturbate' and 'ejaculate': you 'wank' or 'explode'. But our distaste for their words is far more deeply rooted than the words themselves. The snickers I have heard in staff rooms over words like 'orgasm' and 'vagina' show that the problem with sexual language does not start with young people. It begins with us, the adults. We have managed to make available for general consumption so few acceptable sexual words that our ability to talk about sex is perforce severely limited. It is not surprising therefore that few people hold clear ideas about sex and sexuality. You cannot form a considered opinion about something if you do not have a comfortable language with which to do this; and you certainly cannot describe it to yourself or to anyone else. This is why most parents find it impossible to talk with their children about sex.

What is surprising is that people imagine this is a story of the past, not the present. Because teenagers have developed their own aggressive way of expressing their feelings about sex and because advertisers have an equally aggressive interest in the subject, we imagine that sex has become 'mentionable'. This is not so. In eight years of meeting parents, teachers and pupils and in discussing the subject with other sex educators, all my experiences have borne out the fact that, except in the most cursory of terms, sex is still unmentionable. Thus one girl who wanted to ask me . . . what exactly? did so in the following way:

'Miss, what happens . . . if a boy's . . . you know . . . thing . . . doesn't have . . . any . . . you know?'

The answer to that is difficult!

It certainly requires the suspension of all assumptions. The girl *could* be asking about a penis, but she might not be. She may be imagining there are some penes which do not emit sperm, or that an erection is a feat of modern technology and she wants to know if all boys have the same supply of elastic. Or is she confusing penis with testicles? But that may be far too complicated a thought. She may be asking, having seen a baby nephew in the bath, if he is peculiar because his umbilicus does not have a knot in it.

The non-existence of a common sexual language presents problems in many other ways. If you mention the phrase 'making love' to most 15-year-old boys they will put you in the same class as a dinosaur and fall asleep: it has as much immediate relevance as football results from Madagascar. If, on the other hand, you say the Latin word 'penis' to some 15-year-old girls they will behave as if they have been verbally assaulted. When you meet these two groups of people in the same class it is like leading novice climbers through the Alps. At each turn you wonder if someone will get hurt, damage someone else, or if a shout from one side will bring an avalanche down on all your heads. Words, we are told in the nursery jingle, do not break bones, but young people's sensibilities can be cruelly hurt by them. The most difficult part of sex education is 'watching your language'.

Finding a common language for sex is a concern not confined to the classroom. To work out an approved way of communicating the subject which does not offend, alienate or cause misunderstanding is a problem which perplexes the people who formulate school curricula as much as it does the teachers and pupils. This was shown clearly when I was asked to script and co-direct a film on menstruation to be shown in secondary schools, mainly to girls between the ages of eleven and fourteen. I accepted the commission because I thought I would enjoy making a film and because I thought it was a good opportunity to deal with this fairly simple subject in a clear and appealing way. Menstruation is not difficult to explain — it pales into insignificance compared with complex questions like: 'How do I know if I'm in love, Miss?' — but it still creates anxieties for girls whose first period comes as a nasty shock.

The co-director and I worked out a format for the film which we thought would be appealing to young people, and our 'treatment' was approved by the Health Education Unit which commissioned the film. Our plan was to employ teenagers to take part in the film and to find a young actress of about sixteen to be the narrator. So instead of having a doctor, an authority figure, to explain developments during puberty, we would be using an 'older sister' figure. The thinking behind the film took into account what we felt were important issues. We wanted to explain 'periods' in the context of ordinary life and not to have too much fuss made of them; we wanted to have boys in the film to illustrate how they too should know about menstruation; and we wanted to impart as much technical information (how, for example, to use different tampons and towels) and as much reassurance (what to do about period pains) as we could in the twenty minutes allotted.

Given that I am a sex educator, explaining menstruation accurately did not seem very much of a problem; my colleague's task in finding a suitable girl actor and in making animated sequences seemed far more difficult. But that was not to be the case. The lengthy and time-consuming meetings that followed our acceptance of the project culminated, at the end of six months, in a near uproar over the use of the word 'vagina', which the Health Education panel classified as an unacceptable word.

Explaining the process of menstruation without ever mentioning the word 'vagina' is an exercise beyond my skills and aspirations! There *are* alternative phrases: 'the blood falls away from you' and 'when you start bleeding' and so on, but they are misleading and can cause painful embarrassment and incomprehension. No adult who has been present in a classroom, as a colleague was, when a girl who had asked to be excused returned to the room wearing a sanitary towel looped round her ears, so that it covered her nose, would mislead anyone as to where the blood comes from. The girl had been told, in vague terms about 'the bleeding' and so far in her life, the part of her body from which blood had flowed was her nose. She had been receiving some sex education which had told her she would start bleeding soon so, when she felt the beginnings of a nosebleed, she had asked the teacher for a sanitary towel. I admit this is an extreme example of what can go wrong when you use euphemisms and guarded language but it demonstrates the confused ideas which can result.

It was therefore with strong hearts and firm resolve that we fought for our words. But each time we travelled to meet the panel which had commissioned the film we felt more despondent. The Chairman of the Education Unit, a doctor, a teacher, a social worker and the other interested parties were not convinced by our case: that the truth should be told simply and plainly. And in the end, the script contained so many ambiguities and discrepancies that I warned I would withdraw from the venture unless we rallied to some sense. So we scrapped what we had and began again, this time coming up with a script which was a severe compromise, but at least not inaccurate.

This was not easy. In the original briefing session we had examined closely what should and should not be described to 12-year-olds in the area of sex education. We agreed it was impossible to make an accurate film on menstruation without describing why it comes about — and having linked the menstrual cycle with childbearing — how *that* comes about: i.e. fertilization. We had confirmed that the explanation of fertilization should be simple and factual, I on the grounds that there was no time for any more, and they on the grounds that they did not want any more. We were therefore angry to find our severely pared explanation of how a sperm fertilizes an egg struck off the script when we attended what was to be my final meeting. This had happened, it was explained, because the film could not be shown in 65 per cent of schools in the region if it dealt with fertilization.

That there are secondary schools which *insist* on facts about fertilization being kept from their pupils is something discussed in detail later in this book. It is a situation we have had to accept in some schools and at the meeting it was similarly impossible to make ourselves heard. We asked the panel to look at the implication behind their ruling that teenagers should have 'the facts of life' withheld from them as a matter of policy. They said they were sorry, but their hands were tied. When we asked in what way and by whom, they explained that they had gathered advice from head teachers and various interested parties over the months and that it was obviously no use making a film which 65 per cent of schools would not use. We were never given a satisfactory reason as to why this was so; perhaps because the heads concerned found themselves too embarrassed to explain? The panel kept coming back to the word 'unsuitable' and we got no further.

We asked for a good reason why factual information on fertilization should be kept from young people and, since they could think of none, suggested that the head teachers who had advised them should be questioned further. The argument went on at length. We reminded the panel they were revoking previous agreements without which we would never have begun the film in the first place and said we would withdraw rather than have our names associated with a product which would be misleading. By using this threat we eventually kept fertilization *in*, but it was a brief victory. The wrangling which followed was even more wearying, and the battle of words was still to come.

In sex education we have found it impossible to explain fertilization to people in puberty, or to anyone else for that matter, without using the words 'vagina' and 'penis'. We may be dissatisfied with these words, but their meaning is at least constant. The euphemisms for them, like 'birth channel' or 'John Thomas' are not appropriate for many reasons: there are regional differences in these terms; the former is often confused with the cervix and in the case of the latter I would not formally use it in case there is a boy of that name in the class. When, therefore, the one doctor in our midst objected forcefully to the word 'vagina' we thought he was appreciating the problem we have with sexual language and listened attentively to what he had to say. A man well used to people's sexual embarrassment had no doubt thought the matter through further than we had. Sadly, this was not the case. Although he disliked the word 'vagina', he could only report this fact. He did not know why he was uncomfortable with it.

We were shocked at the implications of this. We are used to young people finding vagina far too remote a word for them to use easily. We were not expecting a middle-aged doctor who treats the human body daily to be ill at ease with the word without knowing why. (He later admitted he did not like the word, 'penis' either!) I would not have minded, although I would still have resisted, had he wanted to substitute more colloquial words, but his surrogate was, in the end, the coy phrase 'front passage'.

Our searching for words to use could have been comic were the issues involved not so serious. There we were, grown people, stumbling around like babes on an abacus. The thought was sobering that we were all, in our various ways, in charge of the minds and bodies of adolescents. As we sat there 'front passage' was eventually thrown out in favour of a variety of words, including 'hole'. It was at the point when they reached the phrase 'middle passage' that I had once more to remind them of the existence of some basic ground rules. It is all very well discussing the merits of words in a committee room — or rather it is not, but we had to suffer it — but what do they mean in the classroom? I explained how I saw a number of girls who were caused considerable anxiety by the expression 'three passages'. They thought they were abnormal because they could not find a third passage (the urethra) and others were precluded from using tampons for fear of inserting them in the wrong place. I said the phrase, if unaccompanied by a lengthy explanation, for which we did not have time, was misleading. So after much sighing and shaking of heads we came all the way back to 'vagina'.

It was then the turn of the poor penis. They went through 'sexual organs', and the odious 'private parts' after tea, by which time the clock was beginning to be a bigger arbiter than anything else in the room. It was daunting to realize that three hours into a meeting, ten well-paid and highly trained people had all been directing their considerable talents to finding substitutes for two commonly understood words — and what is more, they had failed. To great reluctance, and even more sighing the word, 'penis' held its own and was put back into the script.

Having won back our words we felt chastened at what we had been a party to, but relieved to have at least succeeded. 'Any Other Business', however, had another tussle in store for us — the *description* of fertilization. Yes, we could say a man had a penis, yes we could say a woman had a vagina, but what we could not say was that ever the twain should meet. The bit where we had described in terms of making love, the depositing of the sperm in the vagina had to go. Since we had spent a long time making the description as uncontentious as possible, we were at a loss to see how we were to do this; and, although it was the panel who had complained, so were they. They must have begun to see how we earned our money when they tried to work out a way of describing the event without actually referring to it. In the end it was the doctor who came up with a phrase which suited everyone — except the two people making the film. It was: 'The sperm *arrive* in the vagina.' It was, they all agreed, beyond our brief to say by what means.

In idle moments since that time I have diverted myself with the idea of those sperm 'arriving', ending up with a mental picture of a trainload of little fishlike creatures wearing bowler hats with a caption underneath them saying: 'The sperm now arriving at platform four are for Newcastle only . . .' In fact, what appeared in the next version of the script, at which stage I *did* resign, leaving the poor director to face it on his own, were the misleading and therefore dangerous words: 'The sperm *in* the vagina'. In the myriad confusing pieces of information which young people dig up before finally putting the jigsaw together, the notion that sperms are somehow 'in' the vagina is one of the most problematic. At best it is confusing to them, a red herring, and at worst the sort of misinformation which makes it possible for a few girls, believing they are already possessed of sperm, to have sexual intercourse without realizing it is *that* act which makes them pregnant.

The other issue on which I resigned was a question of racial discrimination, I mention it here to illustrate how the calibre of those making important decisions in education should not automatically be relied upon. The film director and I had discussed in the early stages of planning our work how it was important to show some black children in the film. We were both concerned that all the films that we had seen on childbirth and sex education, with but two exceptions, had shown only white people. We were determined that our film would do better. The panel initially accepted this point, but then, for reasons we never understood, disallowed it. The chairman explained this by declaring there were no coloured people in the area. What? we exclaimed, None at all? And if that is so, how do you *know* it is, and why should it make any difference in any case? The chairman was embarrassed, but adamant: he was on a sticky wicket, but determined to stick to it. His part of Britain, he explained, was not 'coloured', and to show any 'coloured' children would render the film unsuitable for use in the region. Because there is no logic in that statement we hoped to win him round by introducing some. We said that even if the 'coloured' population in that area was so low as to pass unnoticed in his eyes (and that it was non-existent we did not believe) it did not prevent us using some black children since everyone knew they were present in Britain. He parried this by saying people in London (meaning us two) did not realize how different the rest of the country was, and added that since the film was supposed to be shown in a certain area it should depict the characteristics of the area. He would not be moved from that.

This explains how a simple film on menstruation can develop into a product which, when you analyze it, is harmful because, by omission it distorts. If one is concerned about the hidden politics and influences which find their way into the classroom, then this film is very worrying. It was eventually seen by us as having two principal tenets: that it was important not to give teenagers accurate information on fertilization and that it was important not to have any black people in it. These were the two points on which the panel stuck to their guns. If one wanted to reduce that to simple terms, I would suggest that the film was therefore obstructive and racist, and that these two factors fundamentally undermined its basic purpose — to inform about menstruation.

Having seen a number of films made for use in schools, it is clear that this is not the only film which suffers from the sort of biases I have just mentioned, and what is particularly disturbing is that individual members of the panel would I imagine strenuously deny being prejudiced. What has therefore occurred is a situation where people who are designated decision-makers and who hold the power of deciding how young people are to receive information, are in such a state of basic confusion that they perpetuate attitudes they do not believe they hold. They are in other words deluded. If challenged, they would be outraged to be told they were obstructing the course of education and, what is more, they would be sincerely outraged.

What is also clear from watching 'educational' films is that some of the basic principles of education are not kept in mind when preparing material from which children are to study. So much of the so-called 'educational' material I have seen is not fit for human consumption. It is superficial, deluded and obstructive to the process of learning. This is illustrated by one of the visual aids I have used. It has been specifically prepared by an organization specializing in charts for the purpose of sex education. On the front page of the chart, which deals with contraception, is a drawing of a female. She is standing naked with her eyes demurely closed, head averted, and is a pretty shade of pink from head to knee. She has no hair, except on the top of her head, no nipples, and her breasts do not obey the law of gravity. She has a figure which would not be rejected by *Playboy Magazine*. She embodies all the traditional male fantasies. Her skin has not a wrinkle, her outline is 36–24–36. She is passive and 'perfect'. I have, however, found a role for this identikit woman and use her as a way of demonstrating what a woman does *not* look like. I introduce her with the words: 'I hope no woman in this room looks like this, and I hope no man expects her to . . .'

This chart does not present accurate information; it is lying or, as some people prefer to call it, misleading. We are not supposed to mislead young people in schools: we are supposed to educate them. And the process of education is a leading out process, not a cramming in one. My understanding of it is that it leads people to be able to fulfil their personal talents for the good of themselves and of the community. If these two objectives conflict, it is important for the young people to be accurately informed so that they are responsible for their own actions. In other words, if they are going to take risks with themselves or others they must know what the social and legal repercussions are. So much of the 'educational' material I have seen distorts, as the chart does, by omission and seems to have been devised for the purpose of continuing half-truths rather than of exploring possibilities for enquiry and learning. If the tools teachers have at their disposal are unsuitable for the work in hand, their work is made unnecessarily difficult.

At home, parents are not faring much better when it comes to helping children to learn about sexual matters. Already, in their families and from their environment, young people have picked up some very confusing ideas about sex and sexuality. Enlightened parents and teachers will have done their best, but alas there are too few people who are comfortable with this subject. And even those who have tried hard will rarely have managed to bring to the subject enough time and expertise to inform properly. So, for the main part, the explanations of sex will have been oblique. Sex by any other name will have talked about 'parts' and 'bit' and 'thingies' and 'watching out' and 'keeping out of trouble'. Armed only with ghosts of messages and a variety of different clues pointing in different directions it is not surprising that teenagers have a far less defined view about sex than we imagine.

There is an absurd vagueness in the way adults describe sex. An illustration of how misleading it is not to come to terms with even quite basic sexual language was shown by a letter which arrived in a junior school staffroom one morning. The 7-year-olds had had a simple lesson on 'babies' the day before. They had been shown through a television programme how a baby chicken hatches out of an egg and, through animated diagrams, how a human baby grows and comes out of its mother's tummy.

A letter from one of the pupils' fathers complained about this, and ended with the cryptic statement: 'My wife was very upset when my son told her about these things. You see she didn't know anything about it.'

One would be forgiven for imagining that 14- to 15-year-olds *do* know everything about it, but they do not. Unfortunately, unlike other school subjects there has, up to now, been no well-defined curriculum for sex education and, as I have discussed, no acceptable language in which to contextualize it. The Latin-derived language which I, as a teacher, use, is rejected by most young people in favour of their own slang words, and if I tried to teach with it, and with nothing else, my audience response would be minimal. Yet I cannot simply jettison the 'correct' words because young people do not like them — that too would be against educational principles. But you can see that the problem is considerable. Add to the task of finding an acceptable language the problem of communicating by it, and you might understand how we feel when we walk into a classroom. Our subject is contentious; we are not regular staff members who know who the 'difficult' pupils are; our brief is to 'do it all' in three lessons, and before we can even get started, we have to find a language with which to communicate. Some orders are tall: this one has the proportions of a leviathan.

A method of approach charming in its simplicity and wisdom, called 'The Word Game' was thought up by a fellow sex educator as an answer to being launched into a new class. The Word Game is a stratagem which uses negative forces to positive effect. It is also easy to use, flexible and, in the years I have employed it, it has never failed to enlighten and to entertain. What it entails is an exercise in communication which allows the teacher and the pupils a chance, in a lively and informal way, to look at the words we use and our reasons for using them.

I write on the blackboard the words I am going to use during the course of my visits — words like 'penis', 'vagina', 'menstruation', 'masturbation', 'sexual intercourse', 'menopause', 'contraceptive' — and ask the class what words *they* would use instead. As a teaching aid this provides you with a way of involving all pupils in a spontaneous, but controllable exercise which allows them to have *their* say with *your* guidance. It is an opportunity for them to come out from behind their smokescreens and make themselves heard, and it is an opportunity for me to hear and to know where they are. It is also beginning at the beginning — with what your pupils already know. And while that may seem a simple point to make it is so often overlooked. If you start with what someone already knows they have a foundation to build on, a means of acquiring more information. If you do not do this the process of learning is slow, uncertain and doctrinal rather than educative.

The best description of the Word Game I can think of is by Peter Martin, a journalist, who was commissioned to write an article on sex education for the defunct *NOW!* magazine. He came to two of my classes and the following account appeared in the June 1980 issue:

'All I can hope to do is to make it a little better for the children than it was for us', says the visiting speaker, a woman in her thirties, trained by the Family Planning Association. The headmistress has allotted her just three hours — two ninety-minute sessions — to provide a mixed class of fourth-year students with sex education. Topics to include human relations, sexuality, contraception, mastur-bation, VD, abortion and the exercise of personal respon-sibility.

Class 4B's form teacher, a chap of about the same age as the visiting speaker, initially responds as if she were from an untouchable caste. Cranky with embarrassment, he says hello like goodbye and elects to sit at the back of the classroom. The speaker is thus left to make her own first acquaintance with the children, twenty-five or so 14- and 15-year-olds of all shapes and sizes. Whatever it was they were told in advance, their mood is awkward with trepi-dation and larkiness.

First the speaker sounds out the levels of knowledge and misconception facing her. 'Can anyone tell me what re-production is?' she asks. 'Like with rabbits, Miss?' someone says. 'It's contraception, Miss,' says a girl. Patiently the speaker unravels the girl's mystification until the class is in the clear.

About twenty minutes into the lesson, the speaker writes 'sexual intercourse' centrally on the blackboard. The class erupts with snickers, hoots and general rumbles. It is a prime response which the speaker acknowledges with an empathetic smile. The form teacher drops his eyes.

'All right,' she says, 'does anyone know any other words for this particular activity?' Big Henry, a lad already terrible with masculinity, mumbles: 'Ucking'. 'Fucking, yes,' says the speaker, cool as a cucumber, and writes the dread word upon the blackboard. 'Any others?' Poor Henry is flabbergasted, all his internal security systems momentarily blown away. Not only has the school not fallen down; not only has this woman not been paralyzed by his brute bravado; it doesn't even look as if she intends to punish him.

'Making love, Miss,' from a small girl in the front row. 'Making love, yes', says the speaker, chalking it up.

'Er, Miss, screwing, Miss', offers a lad named Mick. 'Screwing, yes,' and again the speaker chalks it up with no sign of approval or disapproval. There then occurs a small but remarkable event in the genealogy of morals. Mick registers in his expression the fact that the word 'screwing' is a bit smutty and that it was *he* who had uttered it. At first, the responsibility appears to appal him. Moments later, however, he pipes up with: 'Excuse me, Miss, if, erm, fucking is a word for making love, how come it's a *dirty* word as well?' The word *dirty* said with huge indignation. The speaker opens her hands to the class.

'Because some people like sex and some don't,' says Mick.

'Because most people think sex is dirty,' says a girl who's clearly put out that they do.

'Because grown-ups are unhappy,' says a little lad, flatly.

'Because. . . . Because. . . .' Big Henry's hand slowly winds into the air. 'Because sex is to do with feelings and stuff,' he says, 'and because sex gets people angry.'

'Why would that be?' asks the speaker.

'Because they're embarrassed,' says a girl.

'But why?'

'Because,' says Henry, '*because* of feelings and that. Because it's the hardest thing to understand your *feelings*.'

'Exactly!' says the speaker. She now has her cue. 'What we're all here for today,' she smiles around the class, 'is to try to sort out those confusions.' She spells it out: 'It is confusion and worry and things we hardly know how to think and talk about which can mess up our lives, which can stop us from knowing for sure what's good for us and what's bad for us, which prevents us taking proper responsibility for our whole lives.'

It is a lovely moment. The children look around at one another. For one thing, they are not the mucky-minded swine they believed themselves to be until five minutes ago. An exorcism of sorts has taken place. Much demon potency has passed clean out of the words on the black-board because, as words at any rate, they are now fully acknowledged to be part of everyone's experience.

Attention calms and broadens and the energy now at large in the class makes for an extraordinary quality of engagement between speaker and children. They want to be able to make better sense of the confusing hell which is adolescent sexuality, real and imagined, and the very creation of that opportunity has been their own triumph. Over the remaining hour and the ninety minutes of the following week, the speaker manages to 'do' all her topics, but in such a manner that the form's teacher, at the very end, is moved to speak, 'Amazing . . . asking the children what they know and using that as a basis for . . . I mean, I really think we ought to do more of that in class, incred-ible. . . .'

The Word Game is a simple way of establishing rapport with twenty-five strangers, but it does far more than that. It lets pupils know something which teachers are usually at pains to keep from them — that education is a process of discovery through participation, and that it is an individual process, not a mass exercise. The Word Game is also an opportunity for everyone to let off steam at the beginning of a lesson, a time when young minds, not to mention tongues and bottoms, are wriggling with unresolved energy. As a by-product, it is also a useful way of coping with the saboteurs who are present in most classes. If the word, 'fuck' is written up on the blackboard to begin with, somebody who wishes to bring about your downfall cannot make much of a disturbance by hurling it at you like a stink-bomb during a lull in the proceedings.

It is a dubious capacity at any gathering to know more words for sexual intercourse than anyone else! So although I have heard most of the words before, it is important to keep quiet about it. It is important that the words are given to me, not supplied by me. And they are supplied by another simple, and much underrated principle — honesty. I merely explain to the pupils what my problem is: that I have come unequipped with a mutual language we can use. I therefore ask if they will go through an exercise, or play a game with me, to see if a language will emerge that we can all feel comfortable with. It is another indictment of education as it is generally perceived that the young male teacher mentioned in Peter Martin's article was not the first to exclaim: 'I see what you're trying to do: you're trying to get them to think. We don't leave much room in the curriculum for that.'

There is, however, room for thought from what the blackboard shows up at the end of a sex education lesson. There would also be room for apoplexy if you left the words on the board for anyone else to find. There is no shortage of them, and, in the early stages of the game they usually have only four letters. Some classes are a little reticent to speak their minds to begin with, but they soon warm up when they realize that you are in earnest, that you really do want to hear from them. I suppose it is not common for teachers to portray themselves as vulnerable and I should not mind, rather the contrary, if the sight of me stuck out front without a language at my disposal evoked sympathy in some quarters. We are, after all, in the same boat over this language business, and concern for my plight might become a communal concern.

Eventually, some of the words given are obviously silly, but in order to keep to the spirit of the exercise, they have to be treated, by the teacher at least, as if they were sincerely meant. So anyone who shouts out the phrase, 'tree trunk' for penis has his word treated the same as anyone else's. It is not up to me to reject words I think are unsuitable in an exercise which is about trying to find a common language: the language would not be common if I issued instructions about its content. Tree trunk is, in fact, a good example of how wrong it would be to do other than play the game according to its first rule — which is that everyone deserves to be heard. The first time this phrase was shouted out in a class, I had never heard it before and because, when you are dealing with up to twenty-five strangers, you cannot give everyone the quality of attention they need, your mind is somewhat overloaded.

So, caught on the hop, my initial reaction, which I concealed from the class, was one of annoyance. This phrase must be the result of someone being obstructive. And that could well have been the case. In which case, the writing of a preposterous word on the blackboard along with the others, clearly sincere, is a lesson in how a group can be self-regulating. Peer pressure being what it is, other pupils' annoyance is far more effective than mine in letting people know they too have to play by the rules. But, as I was writing this phrase down, I realized that I had been slowwitted: tree trunk is a hyperbolic way of describing the power of the penis and as such is an interesting talking point. So I asked the boy who had given me the phrase why he had used it, and in essence his answer was what I had imagined: 'because it's big, Miss.' To which I replied: 'But not all penises are big. And how can a penis be called a tree trunk and a "prick" [already up on the board] when one suggests it is enormous and the other implies it is tiny. Which is it?'

If it does not seem advisable, let alone crucial, that this sort of discussion takes place in a classroom, then I wonder where else it does take place. That it *should* is, in my opinion, evident. Since a fair proportion of most teenage boys' time is spent on penis preoccupation it seems negligent and churlish not to talk about the subject that is of so much concern to them. Neglecting the subject only reinforces young people's idea that adults are not interested in them, or the idea that a penis is not wholesome since it cannot be discussed. If the wheat yield of the Prairies is part of the school syllabus, a discussion of personal fears is surely not out of place in any system designed to educate and enlighten. If enabling people to mature is indeed one of the purposes of the school system, then a lesson of this sort should be compulsory.

The effects of such a talk are immediate. You would have to see the constrained but obvious relief on some boys' faces to appreciate just how much adolescents do suffer from the bullying and barracking of classmates and to remember what an intensely competitive time these years are. The idea that it is not the size of a man's penis which gives a woman an orgasm is not new to some of them, but it has, at last, become believable. And much less believable now are the boasts of the boys who are the ringleaders of the 'men with big cocks rule the world' club. For them, the game is suddenly over.

The most common objection parents, especially fathers, have given to sex education is: 'I managed without it, why shouldn't he?' Privately, you may imagine he has not managed very well if he has to be so ungenerous, and publicly the answer goes something like: 'Don't you think you may have done even better with a little help? Isn't there always room for improvement in the quality of our lives?'

Another objection is: 'He will find out sooner or later without your help' ('help' here being a euphemism for 'hindrance').

This statement is obviously counter-educational. It is our job to inform when information is requested, not put obstacles in the way of learning. Why should a child be expected to spend five years finding out something which could be explained in five minutes? Knowing that we know, but will not tell, it is not surprising if we are disliked by young people for our lack of co-operation in their quest for information. And if we put up obstacles for them, we can hardly complain if they kick them over, or take longer to complete the course — that is become mature less quickly than we want them to.

Perhaps it is ignorance of the means of passing on this sort of information which has hampered us in the past. With no sanctioned language in which to have a discussion, it is not surprising the discussions have not taken place. Teenagers are so embarrassed about our sexual words that I would not, in my estimation, be able to teach sex education without the use of the Word Game. If I went into a classroom and began something along the lines of: 'Today we are going to begin discussing sex education. For you to understand this subject there are certain important facts you must know. . . . Now, the erected human penis . . . [at which point there would be bursts of uncontrollable sniggers] is approximately seven inches long and . . .' my teaching life would be short.

The Word Game may last for between twenty minutes and an hour, depending on how many stops you make along the way, and it is an invaluable exercise in communication on many different levels. Initially, by doing the pupils the courtesy of asking for their words, by consulting them about their education, one has invested them with a status which they appreciate. Because I have paid serious attention to them, to their words, they begin to reciprocate and to trust me.

I have learned so much from the young people I have been with that it would be correct, in one very important way, to say that they have taught me everything I know, for in consulting them I have been taught how to teach them. This has been made possible by there being between us a way of communicating where my ego and their safety are not at stake. I have not been out to demonstrate my superiority, so I have been no threat to them.

In my classes, I make it clear that I do not consider myself in any way 'better' than the people I teach and pupils of all age-groups respond positively to this. My own schooling was impoverished, and because of this, I especially enjoy being involved with young people in a joy of discovery and learning which I did not experience at their age. Those moments of joy enrich other areas of my life, particularly relationships with young people outside school, and these in turn reflect back into the classroom.

What may be evident to pupils, because of all this, is my enjoyment of teaching which comes directly from my enjoyment of learning. This brings me full circle. I ask children about themselves because I enjoy learning about them and from them. However much I already know, I have never yet been into a classroom where I have not learned at least one thing more, even if it is only how *not* to approach something. Lest any teacher reading this imagines this is impossible, I am also aware that what I say is possible because I teach part-time. I have no doubt that teaching five days a week in the immediate way I do now would exhaust me: but immediate is the way it is. This immediacy helps to make use of all the energy in a classroom; it is a form of engagement which has its advantages and its risks. You have to think fast on your feet, but then good teachers do that. I teach on the basis of pooling resources, communicating and provoking thought. The Word Game is a way of doing all these things.

The response of individual pupils to the Word Game varies considerably, although the game is unwaveringly popular. Some pupils are reluctant to begin giving you their words until you have given them some encouragement, some sign that you are sincere. Others are more boisterous in their approach and ready, as if they have been waiting a long time, to ask why adults will not let them use the words they want to. The word 'fuck' is a particularly interesting one to take up. They are surprised to learn its original meaning (sexual intercourse) and are at first nonplussed to understand why a word which meant making love is now a swear word. Some pupils in the class are nothing short of delighted to hear a teacher use the word; others may be sullen; a few will be embarrassed, and some shocked to hear the word used openly. But the over-riding reaction is one of relief and approval.

Again, the word is much bandied around in the playground

and they are pleased to bring the words they use in the play-ground into the classroom to try to narrow the gap that lies between those two hallowed and unhallowed grounds. The playground is a powerful place and should, I think, be studied more often by those seeking information about ways of helping young people. The classroom has, potentially, far more power, and by bringing playground words into the class you are not turning the room into another playground, but using it as a way of influencing life in the school yard. It is not surprising, therefore, that under the scrutiny of the class*room* some of the playground words lose ground, some are revalued and others are kept, as being descriptions of what people really mean. Examining the words has stripped them of some of their un-wanted potency, making them ordinary rather than extraordin-ary, and under these conditions only the ones which still mean something at the end of the day have much chance of being retained.

It is a pity, therefore, that most adults still react to the word 'fuck' in a way which makes young people all the more deter-mined to use it. The word has power in any case and, by playing our hands badly, we have allowed it to become martyred. This is a point we discuss quite frequently in the classroom. We discuss what might have happened to make it a swear word, who or what makes a word acceptable, and many other issues surround-ing the use of this and other words. We wonder why very few of us are comfortable with the word 'breast' and wonder what else we can call 'mammary glands'. Most young people dislike the word 'tits', 'knockers' is only acceptable among a few, and we try and find out what it tells us about breasts themselves or about us, but we cannot find a word we agree is generally acceptable. By this time, the embarrassed people in the class have realized the floor has not swallowed me up; those who have thought a teacher should not be part of such a discussion have usually changed their minds, and the would-be hecklers are too damned interested to carry on pretending that they're not.

Since every discussion in every class I have been in takes a different form, depending on who says what, after the writing on the board one can end up in any number of different places in the course of a lesson. You might discuss the etymology of 'fuck'; the women's movement from the words you are given for 'vagina'; male aggression from the words you are given for 'penis'; or we might end up working out the other ways open to us of communicating more easily. Another facet of the game which makes it so flexible is the variety of words you may put up on the board. There is no reason, if given the time, why you should not put up dozens of words you would like discussed, ones like 'prejudice', 'abuse', 'tenderness', 'parenthood', and numerous others. From a discussion of these words you would discover a range of attitudes from which the class may learn in a way it would not do if you simply wrote a list on the blackboard which went: 'The characteristics of being a good parent are. . . .'

Some of the words and phrases you are given are, in any case, a credit to their inventors. 'Arsenal's at home' was an inspired way of describing one male football fan's understanding of menstruation, and 'easy rider' quite an original term for a sheath. But it was a boy in a class of not particularly high achievers who gave us one of the biggest laughs to come out of the Word Game. In order to encourage some signs of life in their midst, the class teacher, who had stayed in on the lesson, had decided that after the lesson the pupils should write down, anonymously on pieces of paper, any questions they wanted to ask. This would get them thinking, writing, and it would prevent any of them being embarrassed if their question was one of which they were ashamed. I left at the end of the lesson and returned the following week to find a good-humoured form master greeting me in front of the class with the following words: 'Funny lot these are, Miss Lee. I don't know what to make of them.' He then went on to tell me, to the obvious amusement of everyone else, what had happened after I left the previous week.

He said: 'They were writing down questions for you and since some of them were having a bit of difficulty I said to them: "If you can't spell Miss Lee's words, use your own." [Mine had disappeared from the board as I left.] "If you can't spell the word penis, use cock instead.".

He then said: 'This lot just fell about. You'd have thought the school had been set alight. So I said to them: "Wait a minute, you were okay when Miss Lee was using these words. Why do you have to behave like this when I use them?"'

One boy had answered straight away. He said: 'She's qualified, Sir, you're not.'

With a mandate like that, how can we fail to serve! All too easily it seems. As a prelude to educating someone the method of finding out what they already know is not a new one; but in my own school days it was certainly not used as a courtesy, more as an imposition. The written tests and the teaching, seemed unconnected with what one knew. Which it was. The purpose of my education was to kit me out for an examination system, after which, and not before, I would be asked for my opinions, but only if I was successful. Those who did not pass had not earned the right to their opinions. Despite radical changes in policy making and teaching methods, asking young people for their opinions, and taking them into account, is still a minority exercise.

On the rare occasions when one works with sixth-formers there is a chance to make reparation for the fact that thinking is not usually encouraged in teenagers, but it is only a minority of pupils who reach the sixth. We still play the Word Game with 16- and 17-year-olds but in a more sophisticated way. With them it is interesting to discuss some of the words like 'fornicating' — yes, still being used and heard on a radio programme recently to describe a book reviewer's distaste for the subject matter of the novel he was criticising. And what, in the end, is the difference between attitudes which are expressed by words like 'copulating' and 'fornicating' and those which are expressed by words like 'fuck' and 'screw'?

The fact that we have, in the English language, a rich and varied pool of words and phrases to draw from and still have no comfortable language for sex, does I think speak volumes about our true attitudes. Victorianism is not dead; it is not even lying down. While I have to worry about rubbing off words from the blackboard at the end of a lesson (the Geography master is allowed to keep his) while doctors talk about the middle passage, it is going to be obvious to people growing up among these constraints — our children — that there is something about their bodies and themselves which is wrong. It is the principal purpose of sex education that no young person should feel this way.

2 Non-Battering Families

ALTHOUGH I am deeply committed to my work, I sometimes find it difficult to answer casual questions as to what sex education is about. In order to explain what sex education is, you have to tackle the hefty misconceptions that most adults have about teenagers. Adolescents certainly have a bad press! They are thought of as an unendearing lot stranded between childhood and adulthood, a sort of no-person's-land. Even dedicated teachers of other age groups will shudder when you mention 14- to 15-year-olds.

Once you have got over the idea that teenagers are not an alien species, the explanation of what sex education is about is still lengthy. You have to introduce another unusual idea which is that teenagers know little about sex. Most adults believe teenagers know far too much. Although they use four-letter words and sometimes fling out phrases about vibrators and jolly bags this generally indicates sexual bravado rather than knowledge or experience. I have many times encountered people whose loud boasting covered a pathetic ignorance: one such was an 18-year-old boy who attended a youth club where a colleague was working. The youth worker, John, knew this boy as a forceful person with a lot of problems. He was tall, well-built and seemed to spend most of his time engaged in sexual activity of which he talked freely, nay, incessantly. He had 'had' it seemed most of the girls in the neighbourhood and was spreading his attentions as far as his undoubted charm and limited budget would take him. However, one night he approached my colleague with a problem.

'John', he said in his broad Cockney accent, 'I've got something on me dick.'

John, suspecting VD, questioned the boy and eventually took him into his office to see the injured party. It turned out that the boy had a masturbation sore — and the light began to dawn.

'Have you had any intercourse lately?' asked John in a nonchalant fashion.

The boy looked uncomfortable.

'Not lately', he admitted.

'When did you last have intercourse?' persisted John, almost certain what the answer would be.

'Well,' said the boy. 'I've never actually had it all the way like, but' — (this was all said in a rush) — 'please don't tell the others. My life wouldn't be worth living if they found out.'

John and the boy reached an agreement whereby John would keep his mouth shut if the boy would do the same: in other words John would keep the secret if the boy would stop boasting about mythical exploits.

But it is not primarily on tales like this that I base my assertion that teenagers know very little about sex. It is on evidence from the classrooms where I teach. There I find that teenagers have picked up enough sexual words to cover up their basic ignorance, but have very confused ideas about what they mean. You get instances like the girl who talks nonchalantly about 'the pill' but believes you insert it in your vagina, the boy who thinks the word 'lesbian' means prostitute and the multitudes who still believe in the prevailing myth that you get one go free, (i.e. that you cannot get pregnant the first time). Girls continually ask about this, putting it more as a statement than a question. They say: 'But you can't get pregnant the first time, can you miss?' They believe that the hymen protects you, in the way, say, that a diaphragm does, and that it will stop the sperm reaching the uterus. One 16-year-old girl asked the question a slightly different way when she said:

'If you're a virgin, miss, you can't get pregnant, can you?'

I replied that if you never made love you couldn't get pregnant. And she then asked:

'But if you were making love, but the boy didn't go too far, you know, he didn't go all the way up, you wouldn't get pregnant then would you?'

She believed that, if her boyfriend didn't actually break the hymen, it would act as a shield and prevent pregnancy. It is interesting to note here that even the arguments of people who believe, as many do, that sex education should not be taught in schools, fall down on this point of detail. Even if information about sex were given freely at home (which it is not) it would still not preclude the need for sex education.

Because I see so many young people, and because I see them in groups, I am aware of the kind of difficulties they have. If I were a mother at home I might well not know of the 'one go free' myth and with the best will in the world, if I did not know it, and informed my daughter of all the facts relating to contraception, she might still get pregnant the first time. By seeing so many different young people and from having trained in the subject I am more likely than parents to pick up nuances, gossip and rumours that are doing the rounds. There is also the consideration that however good a parent you are, your child may still want independence from you and may prefer to consult someone else. And there is the problem of adult sexuality. If you yourself are inhibited about sex, or embarrassed in discussing it openly, this communicates itself to your children who become ill at ease if you try and broach the subject with them. Far better in these circumstances that the information be received from an adult who is not uncomfortable about giving it.

The adults who say that teenagers know too much about sex are way off the mark. Even if the mechanics of sex were fully understood, and this is very far from the case, they would know not too much, but too little: the letter but not the spirit. Before you can begin in a real sense to give sex education, that has to alter. How can one convey anything about the tenderness of sex by saying: 'This is a penis and this a vagina and this goes in there. . . .' What sex education is about is the staggeringly difficult task of introducing young people not just to knowledge but to the feelings and thoughts that will bring them and their partner the joy, comfort and peace which loving sex offers.

This may be an enrichment which touches all aspects of life, since the feelings involved in sex are feelings which are involved in other activities too. It is a common mistake to forget this and to talk about 'sexual feelings' as if they are a separate compartment from others. And they are not always. It seems to me that a person's sexuality should not be looked at as a separate part of their personality. If it has, by aberration, been separated, it is that separation which causes problems because you are trying to separate what are inseparable.

In preparing young people to talk about sexuality you have the problem that nearly all of them imagine 'the sexual side' of them as being a distinct entity. You also have the problem that they have been ill-prepared for the emotions that are involved in sex. There is no doubt that kindness is a part of good sex, but most adults do not expect, help or encourage teenagers to be kind. Boys suffer especially from this kind of neglect. How many acts of tenderness is a teenage boy shown, let alone encouraged to explore?

Responsibility is a part of sex, even if it is confined to the basic concern of making sure the girl does not get pregnant. Yet how are young people encouraged to responsibility at home? Are they included in household decisions? Are they encouraged towards the idea of accepting responsibility for their own lives? Is the beauty of being a parent discussed? Thinking about all these things it becomes clear that the changes needed to alter any of them could only be brought about if other people would think about them too.

While adults in general baulk at telling young people the facts, those of us who do, are always going to run the gauntlet of public disapproval. It is so easy for moral indignation to be raised against us. Spurious statements attacking us are commonplace:

'Do you know what these people do? They get kids to think about sex, as if they don't think about it enough anyway. . . .'

Yes, we do ask young people to think about sex, but in order to try and raise it from a lustful into a considered, informed and caring activity. You cannot do that without asking people to think about it. Having asked young people to think about it, I cannot then expect that all the thinking should end up in the same place. If for example, a young person decides from a knowledgeable standpoint that he or she wishes to have a sexual relationship I can question that decision, but I do not consider that I should necessarily try to alter it. There have been a few occasions when, after a class, people have told me directly that they are already having sexual intercourse. I have to say that on none of the occasions did I feel it was seemly to 'scold' those concerned. One was a girl who was only fourteen. I met her while teaching in an all-girls school. The groups were small, and she was one of ten girls. It is easy, with groups that small to form a fuller picture of people's personalities, and though so young this particular girl was remarkable for her maturity. Some of the girls were giggly and since one of them had a Saturday job working on a stall selling pornographic magazines, sexual misinformation was rife in the group. One such 'experienced' lady kept on asking questions like:

'If it's so big, [the penis] how does it all go inside you, Miss?' . . . 'There's a picture in one of the books, Miss, where he can't even fit it in his trousers. It hangs all the way down his leg and nearly reaches his shoes.'

This kind of statement was met with peals of laughter from some of the other girls and a certain amount of ribbing from 'Do you think he wears special trousers?' to 'You won't catch me doing it with someone like that.' But one particular girl smiled patiently at these antics and used her obviously respected position in the group to say things like:

'Don't be daft, Sandra. You know those pictures aren't real'.

After our third session together, she approached me (to my surprise, for she seemed such a contained young woman) to ask if she could have a word in private. What she wanted was contraceptive advice. She had been making love since only a few months after her thirteenth birthday. Her boyfriend had been using the sheath for the past fifteen months and she thought it might be advisable for her to go on the pill. Her mother had agreed she could go on the pill, but the girl wanted some 'expert advice' on whether it was safe. Her boyfriend was two years older than she and they made love mainly in his home before his parents came home from work.

What struck me most about the girl, besides the fact that she seemed so sane and balanced for a person of her age, was her reply to my question about whether making love had affected her school work.

She said: 'I think it's done it good. I was bored at school before. Now there's something to look forward to at the end of the day and I don't mind doing homework when I'm happy.'

When I asked her if any of the other girls knew she made love she shook her head adamantly: 'It's between me and my boyfriend, miss. If it starts getting out round school you only get yourself a bad name.'

Did she think it was right that you should get a bad name for having sex? She hesitated: 'With some girls it's right, if they're going with all sorts of people. It's different if you've got a steady boyfriend.'

Another girl who confided in me was fifteen, one of the loveliest young women I have ever met. She talked about her relationship with her boyfriend with a warmth and wisdom which let me know that even had I wanted to make reproving noises, and I did not, they would have been superficial and ignorant in the face of her maturity. She showed me that if you can bring to young loving the thoughtfulness and confidence which we usually don't find until we are much older, and which many of us never find at all, you have something we should cherish not condemn. That young lady had not fallen from grace to be involved in an act which defiled her innocence. She was engaged in an understanding of loving which is rare in a person of any age. And while I know she is an exception, I cannot, after meeting her, state that all young sex is automatically undesirable.

The other person who had a discussion on this subject with me was a 16-year-old boy. He really just wanted to talk. He was, physically, a very beautiful young man who might have played the field to the devastation of every girl he met. He was, however, deeply committed to his girlfriend and wanting to share with me just how lovely this feeling was. The values of our society are such that he did not feel able to share the joy and excitement of his relationship with anyone else. He was eager to learn how to put into words some of his feelings and to reach out further along the boundaries of the tenderness that he had begun to wake up to. He still had a great deal to learn about his own and his girlfriend's sexuality and wanted to be able to ask another woman about some of the things he was still shy of discussing with his lover. I could not for a moment have put him off his searching and questioning.

It is an act of breathtaking delusion and perverseness to continue to treat young people as if sexuality were something of which they need to be cured. We withhold from them information in such a way that, were it done in any other area of learning, we would see it as a hostile and ludicrous act. Because the information has been so sternly withheld, it is sometimes difficult to begin talking about sex without it being a threatening or embarrassing subject. The twin problems of having no easy access to information and of not being encouraged to think about sex, make it difficult for some pupils to begin to discuss sex at all. They feel doubly confused by lack of 'facts' and a lack of facility — in this case the ability to think a subject through.

Yet given the right starting points and some encouragement, teenagers can perfectly well think for themselves. I am reminded of one class in particular. It happened to contain only girls and we had begun discussing what they thought sex education was, or should be about. There were a number of items on the board, including 'contraception', 'how to look after babies' and the word 'relationships'. So I asked them what relationships were about, who they had relationships with and what sort of relationships they would like to have. We began discussing family life and if they would like to alter it. One girl said she would like a home where people didn't shout at each other and her brother didn't beat her up. I suggested the phrase 'non-battering family' to describe what she meant.

We dealt with a few side issues (like the girls who wanted all brothers banished to desert islands!) and a number of other girls said how nice it would be to have families where people did not shout. From there, we started exploring why people shout at children, and most of the girls concluded that children needed shouting at when they were little, but not when they were their age — that is fourteen plus. So I asked when they thought the shouting should stop. Can you say, shout at 7-year-olds and not at 8-year-olds? They saw the problem. They said you had to shout at children to make them do as they were told, otherwise they would be spoiled, but they did not know at what age you could expect the child to be 'trained'.

I put forward the view that most shouting was wrong. I said I thought that shouting at one person in the family disturbed the rest of the household and I said I did not think it was a good way of disciplining, but would instead probably train a child to shout in turn at his own children. The girls were very against the latter point. They saw no other way to 'train' children but to shout at them. I suggested that we tried acting out a family scene. We picked five girls, two to act as parents, one to act as a 15-year-old girl who was pregnant and the other two to act as her brother and sister. The scene was set for the parents to be at home on a Saturday afternoon and for the girl to come in having just found out she was pregnant. The sketch as enacted by them went something like this:

Mother: Where the hell is that girl. I sent her out to do the shopping hours ago.

Father: Why don't you shut up and let me watch the telly in peace. *etc.*

As soon as she walked in she was greeted with comments like: 'Where the hell have you been?' while other voices in the house added to the tone of grumbling and discontent. And when she gave her news all hell broke loose. Her father had to be prevented by her mother from hitting her, her sister called her a slut, her mother was screaming at her for 'bringing all this trouble on the family' and her mother and father were both shouting at each other about whose fault it was. None of the actors was short of words or actions. They were right into it having a great old time and the audience were thoroughly enjoying themselves too. I was only glad that we were in an isolated classroom, otherwise people might have imagined there was a real fight going on.

After the scenario had finished we had a talk about how far it was exaggerated and both the audience and the actors agreed that, in essence, it was not exaggerated at all. So next I asked them to enact the same scene, but this time doing it in the way they would like the families to behave. I reminded them that they had said they disliked shouting in families — except when it was directed against young children who needed training! — and asked them to think for a few minutes before acting the scene in the way they thought people should treat each other.

What followed was very funny. The mother was scurrying around like a dormouse looking for slippers for her dear husband, while he was filled with highly unbelievable comments like: 'Oh, where is our beautiful daughter?' and 'Won't it be nice when she come back from the shops!'

There was much: 'No, you sit down and I'll do that', and: 'No, don't you strain yourself, I'll make the tea', with lots of little pats going on and the general air of a fifth-rate farce.

When the girl came in with her shocking news the mother, without batting an eyelid said in a flat voice: 'Ah, there, you poor thing', which is about as far as the sketch got before being broken up by howls of laughter from both the audience and the participators.

We tried to work out what had gone wrong. The actors said they could not act it because it wasn't 'real life', to which I asked the question: 'What *is* real life then? Is it being nasty?'

We had a very long discussion about the two performances and it was immensely rewarding. We agreed that the second sketch was not at all believable, yet all I had asked them to do was to act a family scene in the way they would like families to behave. Why could they not do it? Why did they find it so easy and natural to play the scene the first time? If the actors could do the first sketch, why could they not do the second? They ended up saying that when they had to shout they knew how to do it, and when they had to be nice, they did not know how to do it. We wondered why not. Why did they only know about shouting?

'Because we're used to it, Miss.'

They began to smile.

So is shouting at children really good for them?

There was a chorus of 'No, Miss.'

'Why not?' I asked.

'Because then they don't know how to be nice, Miss,' was the answer.

'But what could you use, instead, Miss?'

We spent quite a bit of time discussing what you could 'use' instead. We agreed it was possible to explain to children, even quite young children, what you needed from them, and we also agreed that this takes time. It is far quicker to smack a 3-year-old for going too near a hot stove than it is to explain to him its dangers. Another way of introducing a child to what you want from him is by example, and isn't that exactly what we had just learned about. Since children learn mainly by imitation when they are young, if you want a child to be co-operative and loving, then what do you yourself need to do, and be to encourage this? Through this kind of discussion they began to see that bringing up a child requires far more from them than they had been led to believe.

So 'What is sex education about?' Fundamentally it is about enabling people to think and to explore their feelings and to learn to value themselves and therefore others. It is about trying to give people a sense of their own significance from which to make decisions about themselves. One of the ways to evoke thought is through role-play exercises like the one just mentioned, but while schools only allow a handful of lessons in which to teach sex education, it is necessary for a large proportion of the time to be involved in the giving of basic 'facts' about puberty, contraception, abortion, VD and other information which schools require you to provide.

While it is important to provide such information, it is even more important to be involved in the kind of work which is much deeper than that. This is best illustrated by a group of sixth-form girls with whom I was once involved and to whom I gave no information as we would normally identify it. Our hour-and-a-half discussion was about the beauty of being a woman, about the feeling and appreciation of womanhood. The girls were enthralled. No one had ever spoken with them about the importance of self-appreciation, about the joy of self-discovery and the strength and reconciliation this brings. They had never even thought about the word, 'reconciliation' in all its meanings, let alone discovered for themselves what it is like to be reconciled with oneself and one's surroundings. Their feelings about themselves, when we discussed them, were seemingly nonexistent, even though we went into the subject quite deeply. We talked about how they perceived themselves, what they found pleasant about themselves and what they found difficult. After this session one of the girls came up to me and said: 'Miss, it made so much sense, what you said, and I'd never thought about it. I feel really pleased you've come today. It's made a lot of difference to me — and to the others too.'

Making a difference is part of what sex education is about; making a significant difference in people's abilities to understand themselves, and the world we live in. Yet the longest time I have ever had with a group of pupils is six hours.

With one particular group I remember spending two hours talking about contraception alone, mainly because the group let me know how remote this seemed from their lives. When I came to talking about the cap, a girl turned up her nose and said:

'I don't see how anyone could use that, Miss.'
'Why not?' I asked.
'Because you have to touch yourself,' she said.
We spent the whole of that lesson discussing 'touching yourself'.
'I want all of you to put your little finger up in the air,' I said.
In puzzlement, they did.
'Now, put that finger in your mouth, and rub it up and down the side of your mouth.' Reluctantly, they did.
'I gather nobody has died yet,' I said, and 'the texture inside your mouth is very similar to the texture inside your vagina.'

Some of them are won over, but others still mumbled dissent, and from this I learned that the cap presents young girls with a number of other problems. One I discovered from a girl who asked shyly, when I explained that you have to leave the cap in for eight hours after intercourse: 'Does it mean you can't have a pee for all that time, Miss?' And I realized that she thought the urethral opening was deep up inside the vagina, and that if you wore the cap, it would get filled up with urine.

So I explained with a diagram that although you feel you pee through the whole length of your vagina, you do not in fact and that the urethral opening is situated very near the entrance to the vagina. This was another way of explaining that the vagina is not the 'dirty' object that people seem to think it is. Many lessons get taken up with discussing parts of the body and the way society's general opinion of sexuality is reflected in the difficulty we have in talking easily — about vaginas for example. Most of them are too young to remember the time of vaginal deodorants, and they are usually horrified to think that anyone would wish to employ such a thing. A few of them have, however, asked about the toxic shock syndrome which resulted in the deaths of a few American women. This condition was highlighted when some women who were found to be using a particular kind of superabsorbent tampon which has since been withdrawn from the market, developed high fevers. It is believed that the tampon exacerbated bacteria already present in the women's bodies. Actually, the condition can occur from other causes too which have nothing to do with menstruation, although it is not a common complaint. Once again it is, as far as I am concerned, far better to explain fully what toxic shock is about rather than say: 'Oh, there's no need to worry about it. It shouldn't prevent you from using tampons.'

The Age of Consent is another area which raises many questions. Most young people do not realize that it relates to girls, not boys, and some are confused about what it actually means. Many now think this law is outdated, or unfair because it is sexist, and it is then that sex education becomes history, for the law as it stands can only be satisfactorily explained by describing the circumstances and prevailing climate in which it was introduced. It is a story which they find very interesting because it becomes clear how attitudes to sex, sexual 'rights' and sexual behaviour are, for the most part, governed by the era in which you are born. Most of the girls present have no idea they are comparatively fortunate, and I think it is useful for them to realize this. For even as we speak there are still women in the Third World suffering infibilation (the cutting of the clitoris and external genitalia) and the partial sewing up of the vaginal opening in order to make sure they do not discover sexual pleasure.

Another major part of a sex education programme is taken up with the supportive role of giving reassurance to young people about their bodies as they go through puberty. Many young people hide agonies of fear concerning their bodies, and by exploring some of the myths which surround them, you may prevent a great deal of anguish. And you really need to hear the fears over the years and to be responsive to them to realize how many there are. I am thinking in particular of the fear of masturbation.

One boy I taught who began masturbating guiltily at the age of thirteen, found that he started to grow pubic hair a few months afterwards. He was in a state of near terror over this because he believed that he was guilty of so grave an offence that the Lord had seen fit to punish him by making him grow black hair so that anyone who saw him naked would then know what terrible crime he had committed. Fears of this kind are not rare. What is sad is that so many of them are unnecessary. If young people were told fully about puberty, about growth of body hair, about wet dreams, about the clumsiness which sometimes accompanies adolescence, they could be saved from many of the traumas they go through.

And this, at far too late a stage, and in far too short a time, I and other sex educators try and do. We discuss the size of their breasts with girls, vaginal discharge, and anything else I think they may be anxious about — which covers a multitude of subjects. One girl, for example, once asked me if it was true that women with small breasts could not breast-feed. We had a discussion about this in which I offered as an analogy that nobody would suggest that people with small noses couldn't breathe.

Most girls do not know that it is quite normal for one of their breasts to be slightly larger or smaller than the other, or that slight vaginal discharges are not uncommon at any time of a woman's life. I clearly remember the first time I had a vaginal discharge myself. I was in an agony of anxiety for many weeks. I imagined it had to be VD, which I must have caught from the toilets at school, and the thought of the shame and disgrace, not to mention the harrowing experience of visiting a doctor, all contributed to my being in near despair. The fact that I was twelve and had had no sexual experience did not prevent these thoughts. The way I was told about VD it was all around, ready to grab you if you so much as looked at a boy sideways.

It is hardly surprising therefore that teenagers have little time to *enjoy* relationships with one another. They are so used to being surrounded by half-baked rumours that the actual business of having a friendly, unpressured discussion is not easy. There is no doubt that sexual attraction plays a large part in couples forming a relationship, and one of the reasons for discussing sex with young people is to prepare them for relationships, but how can we hope to do this in so few lessons?

One of the many aspects of human relationships of which it is important to be aware, for example, is homosexuality. And one cannot talk about homosexuality without spending time with it, because prejudice against homosexuality is still the rule not the exception. The Mary Whitehouse view that it is a 'curable disease' still takes precedence over the view that homosexuality is an aspect of sexuality.

Because of this, and in deference to the people in the room who may be either male or female homosexuals, it is important not only to discuss homosexuality but also, implicitly, to be talking about partners in sex, rather than men and women, but this is not easy if time is severely limited. The subject of homosexuality is, in any case, a minefield. Many of the boys I have talked with agree with 'queer-bashing' and have themselves been the recipients of unwanted homosexual advances. They come out with phrases like: 'They're filthy, always after little boys.' And while agreeing that it is wrong, and in fact illegal as far as homosexuals are concerned, for an adult to try and use his superior power and strength to have sex with a young person, I also ask the question: 'But what about acts of heterosexual seduction? You're talking as if homosexuals are the only people in the world who try and seduce people younger than them. Men do that with young girls; and what about men who rape women? Why do you consider homosexuals are worse than them?' It is a delicate area, and one which needs time spent on it.

There are many other issues to confront. There is the question of abortion, and all the legal, moral and medical issues which surround it. There is VD to be discussed. Eventually, there is the whole question of the difference, very marked, at this age, between the male and female expectation of sex and relationships generally. The boys tend to have a mechanistic attitude towards sex, and the girls are still romantics.

'Sex is not a pushbutton business,' I explain to one sixthform group. 'Some men seem to have the idea that if you press a woman in the right places she will, like a doll, feel the right things. Well, it's not like that. . . .'

One of the most humorous and illustrative examples of this is the comment of a boy who approached me once and said: 'Miss . . . me bird . . . 'er clitoris . . . well it don't work. . . .'

I should not even have been tempted to ask him if he had

thought of sending her in for a service . . . as it was, I first of all asked him how he knew his girlfriend's clitoris was not working, and from there we went on to discuss the circumstances in which they were making love and the fact that sex is more about feelings than it is about physical activities.

A friend once gave a description of the way men view emotions when he said: 'They're like accidents. They happen to other people. If you're lucky, you never fall foul of them.' The more I thought about it, the more apt his statement was in describing the attitudes of many of the boys I meet, who go to extraordinary lengths to avoid confronting their emotions. They build partitions of aggression or seeming indifference between themselves and the rest of the world so that no-one sees their vulnerabilities. These partitions are dangerous because they prevent both the world gaining a clear view of the person behind them and that person having a clear view of the world. And as far as sex is concerned there are two particularly worrying distortions men present us with: aggression generally, and rape in particular.

What appals me is that these subjects are usually not discussed throughout the whole of a boy's education. I have never known one boy who has been involved in a meaningful discussion about rape during any part of his schooling — or anywhere else for that matter. How are we to prevent rape statistics increasing even further; how are we to start tackling the myth that boys have handed down to them — that aggression is necessary to virility and that women enjoy it — if we do not discuss the subject with teenage boys — and girls? It is only by discussing it that boys bring out their true feelings, and it is only when this happens that you have a chance of enabling them to understand and to accept responsibility for their feelings rather than to ignore and become victim of them.

For teenage boys, sexual experience is mainly something to be cheered about and boasted of. It requires a fair amount of work to introduce them to the idea of rape as a violation and a tragedy, as something which they can *feel*, rather than just acknowledge. And this again is quite often achieved through role play.

I ask a girl to pretend she is a 15-year-old who has been raped, and who is appearing in court, and I ask a boy to 'defend' himself against the charge. We appoint two legal counsel, one for the girl, one for the boy, and a judge, and the rest of the class act as jurors. This works well as a format, for I stress to the watchers, the jurors, that it will be up to them to decide the outcome of the case and they will be required to give reasons for their decisions. In this way, nobody takes a purely passive role.

What is interesting about this particular role-play is that never has the boy been found guilty by any class, whatever the circumstances presented, even when I, as has happened a few times, take the role of the girl. This is partly because no girl, except for myself, has ever been able to act the role of a rape victim convincingly, and partly because of the awesome amount of prejudice which is displayed. In many cases the girls themselves *automatically* act as seductresses as soon as they step into the witness-box. They too associate being raped with seductiveness, and to act out seduction is easier than to act out distress. Also, there is an assumption on many of their parts that if they have been raped they have in some way deserved it.

But even when there is a non-seductive performance from the girl, the boy still 'gets off'. Comments from the hostile defence counsel are as follows:

'What were you doing out at night anyway? Don't you know decent girls don't go out at night?'

'My client says you wanted it. He says you encouraged him.'

'Your doctor tells me you are not a virgin.'

'This girl slept with my client last year, my lord, so she obviously wanted it.'

'Everyone knows she's a slut. Half the boys in the neighbourhood have had her.'

'Why didn't you scream if you say you didn't want it?'

'Why were there no marks on this girl's body, your honour?'

'Why wasn't she wearing a bra?'

And after that, one by one, we go through the assumptions. Is it fair to assume that any girl who is out at night is not decent? If I am coming home from the theatre at 11 p.m., am I a slut? To which the answer from one of the boys is: 'You should have a man with you.' And then it really gets interesting.

'Why', I ask.

'Because then you wouldn't get attacked.'

'Does that mean that every woman has to have a boyfriend or a male escort the whole time?'

Silence.

'Should the fact that a girl is not a virgin prejudice the case?'

'Of course, miss. If she's not a virgin it means she wants it.'

'Wow,' I say. 'Does that mean that every woman, once she has made love is then every man's property?'

Whenever I have discussed rape there have always been at least a couple of boys who have said: 'But women want it *really*, Miss', or, 'You have to knock 'em [meaning women] about a bit for them to enjoy it.'

I am horrified by these attitudes. They lie so near the surface and I have no idea why we consider them of so little importance. We complain we live in an increasingly violent world, but we are so ostrich-like that we do not tackle this violence before it takes place. Instead we let it happen and shout about it afterwards. Yet it is so much easier to tackle such problems when people are fourteen or fifteen rather than nineteen or twenty-five. It is possible within the space of one lesson to change a boy's aggressive attitude towards sex, just by giving him an awareness of the woman's point of view. Take the following conversation with a 15-year-old boy.

> 'If she didn't want it (rape) she shouldn't ask for it.'
>
> 'Why do you think she's asking for it?'
>
> 'Well, look at the way she's dressed, showing her tits and things.'
>
> We are looking at a picture of what would be called a liberated woman in a well-known women's magazine. I would say she is dressed 'respectably' in a shirt (though without a bra) and baggy trousers.
>
> 'You show your tits whenever you like, and no one attacks you for it. Why should a woman be forced to wear a bra?'
>
> 'She's doing it to get men.'
>
> 'But even if she were doing it to attract herself a boy-friend — and what's wrong with that — does she deserve to be raped for it?'
>
> 'If she's asking for it, yes.'
>
> 'But don't you see what I'm getting at. Rape and sex are not the same thing. Just because a woman wants to find herself a boyfriend, a partner, a husband, why does that

mean she has to risk being raped? Why does a woman saying she wants sex mean in your mind that she has to be raped? And who says that a woman not wearing a bra is looking for sex in any case?'

It would be valuable if we could spend a lot more time discussing the issue of rape, not only because it is important in itself, but because it uncovers so much prejudice and so many assumptions about women — and men. One boy once said: 'Yeah, but it's difficult for a man to understand it, miss, because it never happens to men'. What about homosexual rape? Might this have something to do with aversion to homosexuality. In order for there to be some understanding of rape, men have to be encouraged to examine their attitudes towards women — and themselves — and to examine why they hold such attitudes. One of the things which can usefully be done here is to clip out some newspaper headlines about violence towards women. They are horror stories in themselves. Here are a few random ones:

Bubble and Shriek! Why Peter 'scalped' the missus

Kidnapped — with a Cuddle! Lovelorn Jean snatches blonde

Sex hell of the virgin captives

Porn put youth in the mood for rape

Shame of the Beast who belted Beauty

Bra-less typist 'grabbed' by boss — bust-up in office

Quite often a class, particularly the boys in it, do not see much wrong with these headlines at first — which shows how effectively they have been conditioned to them — and it is not until it is all taken apart and fully discussed that they begin to see the implicit brainwashing in them. So from where do men get their attitudes about women?

Another valuable exercise I have been involved in with pupils is to ask the girls to write a list of their likes and dislikes about boys (of equal length otherwise you get only dislikes) and for the boys to do the same thing about girls. We then read out the lists and get people from the 'other side' (the opposite sex) to defend the points. Conversations have gone like this:

Girl: I don't like the way boys want sex all the time.

Boy:	It isn't only us who want it. You want it too. Only you won't say.
Girl:	If girls have sex, you boys call us names.
Me:	I think she's right. Don't you boys give a girl a bad name if she sleeps around, but if you do the same thing that's okay. What's the difference between the two?

There is, they appreciate, no logical difference between the two.

Another aspect of relationships that it is important to look at is the changing of roles that has taken place, and the imbalances this brings about. We look at what some women expect from men these days, and it seems rather a lot.

'Ladies, your orders are tall,' I exclaim to a group of girls. 'You expect men to wash the dishes, fix the car, do the shopping, look after the baby *and* earn a living.'

'We only expect them to share doing all that,' says one girl. 'That's what we have to do if we get married.'

To discuss the subject of sex education you need to talk about emotions, anxieties, morality, responsibility, parenthood and problems generally. You need to give information about contraception, VD, abortion, the Age of Consent, the law as it relates to homosexuality and all the information that surrounds puberty and reproduction. You need to be sensitive to the different attitudes that people in the class have about sexuality, which brings me to another huge area of work and concern — the cultural differences present in any classroom. They present all of us working in this area with one of our biggest problems, for in some cultures it is important that women remain sexually ignorant, while in others it seems to be equally important that the men show their virility by fathering a child as early as possible.

And here I have mentioned only some of the topics which are covered. There are more. But always the emphasis, as far as I am concerned, is not upon 'facts' but upon feelings. While I am a provider of information, I see my main role as being much broader than that. I am aware that the minds and spirits of most of the young people I meet are so undernourished that they are suffering from a form of starvation. Since I cannot be around, nor can anyone else, to feed them constantly, I hope to be able to introduce them to the idea and faculty of feeding themselves. One of the ways of doing this is to try to enable them to a sense of their own significance; to recognize their capacity to make intelligent informed decisions and to use their own judgement. I would also hope they might realize their capacity to recognize and respond to an ideal of sexuality which transcends the ignorance and ugliness of the one they have passively acquired. If they had a sense of their own dignity, of their own wholesomeness, our time together could be spent very differently. We could really begin talking about tenderness, about the gentle qualities which make concern for others such an enhancing experience for everyone.

Surely what I am trying to do is not unreasonable? I give pupils as much individual attention as possible and encourage them to think about what they are doing in order that they may reach decisions from a position of intelligence, rather than ignorance. I do not see this as gross or revolutionary. But as far as sex education is concerned, I am asked by parents, and even by some teachers, not to teach in the way I have described but to do something quite different. Would a teacher in any other discipline be instructed in this way? It is considered all right, although I wish it were always practised, for other forms of education to be concerned with enabling people to grow, but this is not accepted with sex education, which is considered a special subject. I wonder if it is.

3 The Blind Leading . . .

IS SEX education different from any other education? One could start by asking: 'Should people know about sex?' We are all sexual beings so surely the answer is yes. 'Do people *need* to know about sex?' I would have thought so, since the vast majority of people become sexually active during their lives. Sex is one of the most intimate ways of showing affection for one another as well as the way we procreate. It seems that if we are equipping young people for adulthood, then educating them about sex is vital.

So how can we even consider leaving this important subject out of the curriculum? It must be because we think that sex, unlike other education, should only be learned when you *become* an adult. If we are saying that, then we are denying what we state sex is all about — feelings and relationships. One cannot argue on the one hand that it is wrong for sex to be discussed outside the context of feelings and relationships (which is what it is claimed is wrong with sex education in schools) and yet at the same time suggest that these matters be left aside until someone is eighteen. If feelings are important they need the care and attention that all other learning does. They do not suddenly blossom overnight.

In preparing one for adulthood, sex education is therefore no different from other education. It requires people to learn gradually until eventually the knowledge gained fits them for the responsibilities of adult life. But is knowledge about sex something one should get outside school rather than inside it? The family group is, after all, there to allow growth and development of relationships and feelings. Should sex education be a family affair? This is a difficult question. One of the many reasons why parents are not allowed to keep children from school and to educate them themselves is that many parents would then not bother to educate, others would not have the necessary skills and knowledge and others would give dangerously biased information. And what would happen to the children of parents who did not have the time or skills to educate at home?

It seems essential, too, that the children of parents who frequently quarrel or who barely see one another should have the opportunity of finding out that there are other ways of feeling besides anger and coldness. The other difficulty with leaving sex education to the family is that you could not expect the average parent to have at his or her command the necessary skill to balance the commercialization of sex. While the market place has made sex its business you cannot expect the schools not to make it their concern. If schools do not provide an antidote to Page Three girls, to romantic fiction and to the explicit brutality of the sort of general release films where rape scenes are thinly veiled with hypocritical horror, children are left with a very distorted view of what sex is about.

Another objection to sex education being taught in school is that sex is different from other subjects because it is personal. Even though sex has been made as impersonal as possible in the marketplace, people still feel that we should have the right for our own sexuality to be personal. I could not agree more. It is in an attempt to make sure that sex *is* personal that the subject is brought into the classroom — there is no real education that is not personal. It is in an attempt to stop sex becoming *im*personal either through prejudice, through indoctrination or through market forces that sex education should be provided. We want children to have a personal understanding of sexuality, not a half-picture glimpsed from advertising hoardings and newspapers.

Another problem lies in the fact that I can see from parents' comments that they do not view education as the gaining of understanding by their children, but as an instruction. They think a teacher instructs a pupil how to do things and they therefore think that sex education is an instruction about sex. They see contraception as an instruction on how to have sex and get away with it. What does it say of us, in the teaching profession, that education should still be viewed in this way? They see a discussion on masturbation as a command. I extrapolate this from the number of parents who ask the question: 'Do you tell them it [sex] is wrong?'

They are unable to understand that their children are not ordered to do or to believe things in a sex education class, but asked to enquire. That in itself is a threatening enough prospect. If you give the reply: 'Actually I try and get them to think about sex,' to the question: 'Do you tell them not to do it?' it would be a further threat.

It is obvious that many parents view the child–adult relationship in a strictly authoritarian manner: the adult tells the child what to do. Since true education is concerned with allowing a person his or her own authority, it is very difficult for it to take place when both the adult and the child are locked into a system which goes against education, one in which one person dominates another. And it is unfortunate that people who behave in this way claim they are doing it for the *good* of the person they are quashing. I have in mind the following example.

A journalist colleague kindly loaned me the extensive notes taken from tape recordings which he took when researching an article on sex education in schools. One of the people he interviewed was a woman, a mother, who is so opposed to anyone else having any influence relating to sexual matters on her children or anybody else's that she formed an organization to try to stop this. I was aware of this person's existence through her letters and articles in newspapers and because of some pamphlets in which she set out to undo what she saw as the terrible damage people like me inflict upon teenagers. (I will not quote her by name, since I personally did not interview her, but since she agreed that my colleague should publish her comments I think it is quite reasonable to assume she stands by them.)

In the interview she set out to show that organizations like the Family Planning Association (which trained me) are engaged in a plot to subvert the nation's youth.

> 'Their whole approach towards sex education for the young is geared towards selling them contraceptives . . . first of all you promote the sexual intercourse to create the demand for contraception. And when you've got that you have to have abortion back-up. And they're heavily involved in the promotion of abortion. . . .'

This lady claims the FPA makes a profit from the sales of contraceptives and from abortion referrals which enriches the organizations which she claims are tied up with the FPA, nationally and internationally for the purpose of making money from young people being sexually active. Her arguments continued:

'This ideology is absolutely devilish. These people are madly fanatical people ... they can go into these class-rooms and do untold damage. If you're a nice person you'd be very lost. It's very interesting to see that the FPA want to get compulsory sex education integrated into the curriculum ... [the organization consists of] people who are upholding abortion, campaigning for homosexual equality and so on. There was a meeting [of them] and mostly homosexuals, transvestites and lesbians attended. And they are so dangerous. So much potential harm to so many children. I mean I would really like to see good, responsible people in schools dealing with this sort of thing, someone a child could turn to, people who can give that child honesty and deal with their problems. I'd like to see it. I tried to do it myself but I found it quite impossible in a classroom of twenty or so fifteen-year-olds. . . . [I bet she did!] I don't want other people to talk dirt to my children. Another thing that occurred to me is that it would be awfully easy to get a feedback yourself by titil-lating them [the children] ... these people who have a great desire to talk to children. It's very obvious that they're after something for themselves. I feel there's some-thing distasteful about going and talking sex to children.

Of course they [the children] need to know about menstruation and the basic facts of intercourse. The rest is intensely personal. . . . When there was no sex education people loved each other, they enjoyed each other, some enjoyed sex, some didn't ... it's all just a new way of moving in and taking over. . . . In the classroom they are dangling contraceptives in front of those poor little children's faces ... and the terrible thing about human nature is once you present people with an option you then start giving them all kinds of options — or pseudo-options. Well, take family planning: once contraception was only available to the married, then it was available to the un-married, now it's available to children.'

The vast majority of the children are, indeed, impoverished in some way: spiritually, intellectually, emotionally or physically. Many of them have all these poverties. It is quite an experience to be presented with so much need in a classroom. It requires so much love to repair the damage done to young people by adults who cannot accept their children as sexual beings that you sometimes feel you are setting out on a task which is, before you begin it, impossible.

As for 'dangling contraceptives', there is absolutely no doubt that if you show the same sheath more than once it will dangle: like other objects it is subject to the law of gravity. I can safely say, however, that I feel at my least seductive when standing in a group of people with a sheath 'dangling' from my hand. This is not only something I feel, but it is also felt by those around me. Contraceptives are not alluring to 15-year-olds: they are nasty, surgical-looking, embarrassing, strange objects which they hope they will spend the rest of their lives doing without. But perhaps rather than take all the points which arise from this interview it would be better to look at it in overall terms. And what struck me about this and more especially about the full text of the talk, was what I consider to be a complete lack of appraisal of the needs of 'the child'.

As a contrast, to illustrate fully what I mean, here is a letter written by a teacher, also a mother who was also labelled as a 'child damager', in response to comments similar to the foregoing which appeared in a national newspaper.

'I write in answer to your article regarding 'the pill and teenagers'. I am a health education officer and the mother of a girl of sixteen. I have done a large amount of teaching in secondary schools about contraception and I advise many teachers on the content of their health education programmes which include contraception.

First may I say that in my experience the teaching in schools is excellent. It is done not to further the idea of sex before marriage, but rather because the teachers care very much about their pupils and they want them to have the knowledge to make rational decisions about their lives. At all times the aim is to impart a sense of responsibility to teenagers and in fact 'Responsibility' is the title of a Family Planning Association film that most of our schools use. The theme is one of thinking before you act and of the people you are involving — yourself, your sexual partner, your parents, your school and above all the unwanted baby. At no time, is the attitude imparted of 'visit your local clinic, get the pill and then have a jolly good time with anyone who comes along', but rather that sexual intercourse is an expression of deep feeling for someone and not to be used as a quick thrill.

At the same time it is rather difficult to use the old idea trotted out to me when I was a teenager of 'thou shalt not' because now the answer is 'Why not?' The newspapers are full of news about who is living with whom and when the latest offspring is due to a new boyfriend. Children are not ignorant of biology these days and even a 9-year-old will know that babies are not found under a gooseberry bush. People will say, 'But what about religion?' Do people actually believe that the wrath of God will descend on them because they have sexual intercourse outside marriage? If so, there are going to be a lot of people in trouble. A religion based on fear is but a quasi-religious front for controlling people.

I think the answer to all the parents who are worried that their children may be prescribed the pill unknown to them is communication. It is surprising how many parents to whom I have spoken say: 'My child knows all the facts of life.'

Me: You really have talked to them about con-
             traception, VD etc?
Parents: Well, er, no, but I know they know because
             they have done it at school.

Another father said to me: 'Of course my daughter knows about contraception from school, but in any case she wouldn't do anything wrong.'

Me: How do you know?
Father: Well . . . I suppose I don't, but I hope not.

Why don't these caring parents actually sit down with their children and talk about the problem. Not the 'facts' because that is easy (it's in leaflets and books) but rather: 'I know the pressures are on you and I do understand and if you came to me and say your boyfriend wants to sleep with you I shall not fly into a rage but we will discuss it sensibly and rationally. If you are really convinced that that is what you want to do, then we will go together to the doctor or clinic and see what help we can get. I am your parent and I love you and I would rather be the person to whom you come for help than someone else, however kind they are.'

I have talked to my daughter like this and to many of her friends and to children in schools and I know that they would like to be able to talk to their parents but fear and anger and embarrassment prevents them.

P.S. I really do feel that in many cases young people who have sexual intercourse really are in love and who are we to tell them they are not. I suppose in my letter I have not really stated that I do feel that young people should have complete confidentiality when they visit a doctor, for so many of the young people have no one to turn to for help and I feel would take the risk of pregnancy rather than let their parents know.

I showed this letter to my daughter who says although she can talk to me she thinks that parents have no *right* to know when their children visit a doctor for contraceptive advice.'

The contrast between this mother's attitude and that of the previous person quoted is clear. This letter shows concern for children as they are, not as she would like them to be. In discussion on this point with my colleague he had a far stronger way of putting it. He described the first woman as being 'inconsolable, a person who has never had authority for her own life and who therefore incites authoritarianism in others'. He went on to say: 'At one point I served her up the image of the child. As potently as I could I described to her a child in need. I put to her my case for needing help, I pleaded with her to contemplate the child, and she would not. Her own need to be punitive, her own tragic inconsolability, made it impossible for her to attend to the child. In her scheme of things the child has to go to the wall.'

Since family planning is about having only wanted babies, and not unwanted ones, it is illuminating to explore with a class exactly what 'wanting' a baby means. Why do you want a baby? How much do you want a baby? If you say that you are not going to allow a baby to disrupt your life do you really want a baby, or are you secretly confusing a baby with a doll? The girls in classroom are very quick to pick up on what I mean by that and usually a great deal is learned in questioning ourselves closely about why we want children and in examining the answers. If you accept that every person is born an individual who has different needs and who progresses at different rates from anyone else, it is obvious that each child needs to be catered for individually.

Most teenage girls have been told to 'watch the baby' in the sense of 'keep an eye on him/her', but not in the sense of 'behold him to discover who he or she is'. They are watching to control not watching to understand. Which is not surprising since this is what they themselves have experienced, and continue to experience well into their teenage years. Thus contemplating the child, observing him or her, learning from children themselves what they need are 'new thoughts' to them.

We have not allowed young people the validity of their own experiences and it will be difficult for them therefore to allow their children theirs. This is illustrated by the pejorative definition: 'puppy love'. A 15-year-old who is suffering the emotions of being in love is usually treated dismissively by adults. 'Puppy love' is an adult coinage describing something that is a diminutive form of adult love. Yet the experience of being in love is felt and experienced by the young person as strongly as by an older one. But what is really behind the phrase, 'puppy love' is our notion that as something less than adult love it is something that is felt less. We say that children get over it quickly as if that proves it is not felt very deeply, but the fact that young people have quicker powers of recovery than we do, does not prove that they are hurt less. Knowing that young skin heals quicker than old, does not mean that it is less painful for a 15-year-old to be say, scalded, than it is for a 60-year-old. And where are people to gain authority for their lives except from the validation of these experiences?

On the contrary, for some adults, memories of childhood love and affection retain an importance that has never diminished. One woman told me the story of how she still feels pain over an incident which happened thirty years ago with her boy cousin. They were brought up in the same house together and had shared the same bed for many years. She said:

> 'I was about ten, and he was a year younger when one night he put his hand on my crutch. The only thing I had been told about sex was that I must never let a boy touch me 'there'. I was threatened with nothing short of eternal damnation if I let this happen. I wasn't told why: my parents told me nothing else. So when he did this, I thumped him, turned over and went to sleep.

We continued sharing the same bed for the next year or so, and he never touched me again. Then I moved away. When he was eighteen, he was killed in a car crash and the only thing I could think of was how I'd pushed him away that night. We were very close. We had spent all our childhood playing together. But when I heard the news of his sudden death it was only that night I remembered. And I felt terrible. It still hurts. It was, it seemed, the only unexplained thing between us.

Now I don't know what I could have done that night. People would say 'Well you surely don't think you should have let him', or something equally crude. But that's not what it was about. Had we understood anything about sex, in the way that my own children do, I needn't have been so crude and hurtful. I've no idea how he felt about that night. It may be it was something he always remembered too. And I still hate the knowledge that he died without knowing how much I cared for him.'

Another woman, who married the boy next door — literally – said:

'We were brought up together, bathed together as babies, and went to the same school. We were 'sexual' from as far back as I can remember, but in a secretive way that we kept closely guarded from our parents. We examined each other's bodies when we were about five, and at the age of eight or nine we often fondled each other. I think we agreed to marry from the age of seven, and we were one of the few people who say that kind of thing who went through with it. We didn't actually have sex till I was fourteen and he was fifteen, but I'd watched him masturbating quite a lot before that.

We've been married for nearly fifteen years, and there's no doubt that there's a special bond between us because we've loved each other for so long. When the going gets rough — we do have our arguments — I suddenly see him as a little boy again, and I can't stay angry. I don't know what to say about the sex side of it. I don't feel qualified, since I've only slept with one man. All I do know is that we never felt there was anything wrong between us. We knew our parents wouldn't have approved, so we had a pact not

to let them know. But I certainly never felt guilty. We knew
it was the right thing to be doing.'

The 'right thing to be doing' is less easy to find, however,
when you are an adult making decisions about a young person's
life. But there are, I think, 'wrong' things which, by the recog-
nition and avoidance of them can lead us into clearer areas. And
one of those 'wrong' things is the assumption that adults have a
right to power over children. We feel we must have authority
over children, and that this is necessary in order for them to
learn from us. But I don't think it is. On the contrary, I think the
vertical authority structure we have erected makes life much
more difficult for us as well as for children. In discussing this
with other teachers, some have said: 'Even if we accept that
authoritarianism is wrong, it's practical. How could you work
without it?'

In the short term one does so with difficulty, but I suggest that
in the long term teaching becomes *easier* without it, not only for
the pupils, but for the staff. An example of a situation which
seemed to call for strong disciplinary measures came about with
a group of 'slow learners' of fifteen to sixteen in a mixed class.
We were about fifteen minutes into the double lesson when a
boy six foot tall or more who was sitting near the back of the class
(having refused my suggestion of moving forward in a semi-
circle with the rest of the group) carefully brought out a large
knife. He looked at me as he did so, as he carefully rubbed his
thumb along the blade, and he understood by my gaze that I had
seen the knife. Usually when I am shocked by something I have
a fortunate knack of giving an appearance of calm to conceal the
fact that my mind is working feverishly to try and find a way out
of trouble. So I carried on talking with the group for about a
minute or so until it became clear what I had to do. I said to the
group: 'I have a problem and I need your help with it. A boy
sitting in this class has just let me see that he is carrying a knife. I
want to know what the rest of you feel about this. . . .'

The rest of them wanted to know who the boy was, what he
had the knife for, and why he had shown it to me. The girls were
not happy to sit in front of him, 'when he has a knife at our
backs, Miss', so I gave the boy the option of giving me the knife
or of moving forward into the group. He moved forward. I then
asked about the school rules relating to knives and asked if the

class felt I had a duty to report the fact that one of the boys had a knife. They were undecided. Why was he carrying it?

'He thinks the world's against him, Miss,' said one of the girls.

'It's to keep him out of trouble, Miss,' said another.

I asked the boy himself, who was not forthcoming, except to say that he was in a lot of trouble already. So I asked him if there was a teacher in the school he thought was fair. What was his form teacher like?

'She's okay, Miss.'

'In that case,' I said, 'I would like you and I to go and see her afterwards and have a chat about this.'

I explained how I had a responsibility to everybody in the class to keep them safe, and that he was included in this.

We spent the break with this boy's form teacher, a marvellous person, who was able to throw more light on the incident. The boy, despite his size, had been the victim of more than his share of bullying. He had refused to join a couple of the gangs in his neighbourhood and now they were both out to get him. His teacher was trying to see him through this troubled time, but he felt about as alienated and vulnerable as a human being can do. Halfway through the talk I remembered what I had wanted to ask him.

'Why did you show me the knife?' I asked.

'Because I wanted you to take it away from me,' he said.

This boy was not *demanding* to be punished, he was *needing* to be helped. Frogmarching him to the headmaster's office would have created even more problems for him.

Without knowing where a person comes from, without having a fuller picture of his life, it is difficult to make accurate assumptions about what he is doing. There is no doubt that carrying knives is dangerous: neither is there any doubt in my mind that this particular boy was a victim not a criminal. His form teacher took custody of the knife after a long talk during which this young man was persuaded to the idea that the best way for him to get rid of that knife and all it stood for was to give it away, not to have it taken from him. In allowing him to hand over his knife we had enabled him to unburden himself of a sickening fear — that of killing someone.

I believe that classrooms are about the alleviation of dreads. If the functions of schools are being questioned as often as they should be in a healthy society, I would still put 'the alleviation of dreads' as one of those functions. I would still say that teaching is about encouraging young people to express their dreads and classrooms are about sharing those dreads so that people may learn what it is like to express fear in a safe place. The dreads young people bring into a classroom are disguised as aggression, sulkiness, resentment, timidity — and knives. Their dreads are real. Yet adults, who themselves fear old age, illness, poverty, unemployment, redundancy, loneliness, failure, death, somehow do not know or remember what it feels like to be a child who is afraid. They do not remember what it is like to walk a whole mile detour to get to school to avoid the clique of people who ridicule you every morning because you have large breasts, a prominent adam's apple or ears that stick out. How easy is it to forget the ringing in your ears and the sense of 'please, God, let me die now' when a teacher asks you a question when you have been daydreaming for five minutes and cannot answer it and have to bear the sarcasm and public humiliation that follows.

As a child I hated to see other people humiliated by the teacher. Teachers have altered their behaviour since those days when it was fashionable to behave as if all pupils were army recruits, but the dreads are still there whatever form they take, and they have to be allowed out. The opportunity has to be given to understand and overcome them. But you have to feel safe, or else admitting to your dreads can be what it is for most adults, a way of giving your 'enemies' ammunition against you. Once, in a classroom, we were discussing embarrassment which I suggested was basically fear in disguise, when one of the boys said: 'It's okay for you, Miss, you're the teacher. You don't have to be embarrassed. It's different for us.'

I asked him what he thought it was like to be a teacher with twenty strange people sitting round you all of whom know each other when you are the only outsider. I asked him to imagine what my fears were. He could not. So I asked the other people in the class the same question. What did they think teachers were afraid of? None of them had any idea at all. They thought being afraid was something you experienced when you were young, that it was therefore immature, and that adults, who were mature, were not afraid.

In a sex education class there are no intrinsic rules for us and rules for them, and the alleviation of pupils' dreads is at the crux of another dread — adults' fear that their offspring will become sexually active. It is alarming that children remaining ignorant is not a cause for fear. Innumeracy and illiteracy do not attract the newspaper headlines that sexual activity does. It is not the darkness of illiteracy which worries people as much as the evils of sexual activity.

When you tell a mother therefore that a sex education class is about the alleviation of dreads you strike fear in her heart. The dreads of VD, pregnancy, parental wrath, societal shame and God-given punishment are the staves used to fend off young people from enquiries into their sexuality. If we are taking away those staves what must we be about?

In our own eyes we are about the business of being humane and of educating young people to a sense of their own worth, to a sense of their own dignity. There are enough 'real fears' in the world as it is. The alleviation of the dread of young people that they are somehow basically unworthy, unqualified to join the human race, that they are basically unwholesome, is part of what sex education is about. But in a society that is ruled by fear, that would seem to be an impudent exercise: 'If they are not scared of authority they will run riot.'

If you talk about alleviating these fears with parents, they will invariably bring up the matter of examinations. A father will say: 'It's all very well you giving that spiel. It's all theory. If I hadn't told my boy there'd be hell to pay if he didn't pass his "O" Levels he'd be unemployed now. He has me to thank for that. He'd have loafed around if I hadn't told him what he'd be in for if he failed.'

The idea that you can be frightened into achievement is very prevalent. The child proved he had the ability to pass the exams but even afterwards this parent, like many others believed he succeeded only through threat. Encouragement is thought of as a soft option.

It is a great mistake to say that because we have acted from fear that fear is then a valuable motivator. Fear is a minimal motivator: it makes you do enough to escape sanctions or punishment. It does not encourage you to co-operative and creative activities. And what it does is to hide from us, or to make impossible for us, a motivator which really is valuable — affection.

It is a sign of how bereft we are that a teacher dealing in human relationships should have to hide the fact that she teaches with affection. Should the subject of relationships be dealt with in any other way? If you use the word 'affection' in connexion with teaching you are laying yourself open to criticism. As a teacher of young children you are allowed to show affection. Why do we consider teenagers not deserving of it? Is not the answer to do with sex? Young children may be loved, cuddled and played with because they seem nonsexual. Adults may be cuddled and played with as part of the foreplay of lovemaking because they are established sexual beings. Teenagers, however, are unestablished sexual beings, and it seems, therefore not deserving of the respect that an established sexual person is allowed. The thought of sexuality in young people stirs up fearful emotions in adults and it is these which send children to the wall. In order to keep young people from sex we keep them from affection, which is to suppose that all affection is sexually laden, which of course, it is not.

While we reject the sexuality of young people and stick our heads ostrich-like in the sand, a generation will grow up without any real assistance from us. They will be no better prepared than we were to find a way in life, mistakes will continue to be passed on from generation to generation. I do not consider Dr James Hemming exaggerated when he said that sex education is about the future of the world. Young people are growing up with little hope of loving, since they have not been unreservedly loved. If they grow up in fear, they in turn will transmit that in the fearful acts which make wars, race riots, poverty, greed and starvation inevitable. Education as a whole would be transformed if the mental and emotional blocks which prevent adults from accepting the fact of adolescent sexuality, could be dissolved. Adults themselves need to learn before the children can be educated.

Sex education is about the future of the world because it provides young people with an opportunity to grow which is usually denied them. If instead of bringing up children to our blind habits we allowed them opportunities to do what they are able to do well — to see for themselves — then they would demonstrate the 'rightness' of our facilitating this by becoming, quite simply, people with a breadth of vision we do not possess.

4 Healthy Respect?

IT WAS almost by accident that I first started examining with young people the word, 'respect'. The notion, as something which is fundamental to relationships, is intrinsic to a sex education programme, but the word itself did not arrive on the blackboard until I had been teaching for more than a year. It came up near the end of a lesson in which the pupils had consumed energetically all that had gone before and were obviously ready for a *real* challenge. Unwittingly I gave it to them. In retrospect I realize that even before the 'T' was crossed the hairs on my spine had picked up a remarkable change in atmosphere which, when I turned round from the board, was transmitted by the faces around me. The group who had just given me 'Arsenal's at home' to describe menstruation looked as if the thought uppermost in their minds was escape. And in view of what I learned from them in the next fifteen minutes I can hardly blame them. It was, in essence, this: that of all the words I had written on the board so far this one was the 'dirtiest'. It was at the door of this word that they laid much of the blame for the unhappiness in their lives: without it who knows how their days might have been transformed?

Their reason for disliking this word was a revelation to me for which I will always be grateful. It opened up avenues of enquiry which I am still exploring and which have led me to an understanding of what it is to be an educator, as opposed to a teaching technician. For them the word symbolized adult oppression and in putting it on the board I initially joined sides with their oppressors. I put it this strongly because I have never since seen a class move so abruptly from one mood to another. They had begun to like and trust me and suddenly they were not so sure that they had been right to do so.

What this class told me about their understanding of the word, 'respect' went as follows: it was a form of tyranny to them because they had been used to it as a one-way transaction; it was a way that adults exerted authority over them. As young people they were required to pay respect, but they were never given it. Adults demanded respect from them, just when they felt like it, but they were never paid any in return. They were used to hearing of it as part of a tirade which begins: 'You'd better learn some respect, my girl, or else. . . .' They had never heard it as part of a conversation which starts: 'We respect your feelings that you love this young man. Will you respect ours and understand that we are worried because. . . .' They were used to respect being demanded of them, sometimes at the most inconvenient times, always regardless of their feelings and never as part of a two-way transaction. It was not surprising, therefore, that the words and phrases they gave me for 'respect' were: 'ordering', 'listening to'; 'being told what to do', and 'keeping your mouth shut'.

Ever since that class I have made sure that the subject, respect, is an explicit as well as an implicit part of lessons and, except with the occasional sixthform group, the response to the word has always been similar. It has been marked by discomfort, hostility, or a spirit of non-cooperation. Nevertheless, by taking time to get to know the pupils, a lesson in respect does, in fact, take place. In the classroom we have paid one another attention: by listening to one another's words and learning from them. The trouble is that none of the proceedings would show up well in an examination paper; and overheard cries of: 'Can we play the dirty words game again, Miss?' would not endear me to parents either. And I do not have a leg to stand on in defending myself, unless someone takes the time to try to understand what is really going on. Beginning an explanation with: 'Well, actually, The Word Game is an exercise in respect . . .' would understandably carry no weight with a mother who has just come storming through the school gates demanding to know why her son spends his time in school learning how to swear.

The problem of respect is not, of course, confined to the relationships between children and adults. It exists so frequently in adult relationships, which children copy. And what is worrying about being involved in sex education is that, since the subject itself is not respected, neither are sex educators. An example of this was illustrated by the time a colleague was asked to visit the vice-principal of a school after teaching there. It is a school we visit regularly and the head of general studies, who invites us in, is always courteous and, in fact, enthusiastic about our work. He apologized for having to 'summons' my colleague, and she soon realized why. On meeting the vice-principal for the first time, he told her he had listened outside her door for a few minutes and had not liked what he heard. It seemed he had the feeling, from his few moments of eavesdropping, that they, the pupils, were being told about contraception as if it were a fact of everyday life rather than something only to be used by married couples.

My colleague was disturbed by this meeting. She explained how unfair it was to be overheard in this way and how easy it is to take remarks out of context. She explained that it was certainly not her desire to encourage young people to use contraceptives, but neither did she feel it is correct to tell them they may only use them if they are married. This bothered the vice-principal even more. He said that contraception should only be taught within this context. And here we have a problem. Unless the work we do is respected, other teachers will feel they have the right to interfere in our teaching. My colleague backed down from saying this, or anything like it, because she did not want to jeopardise our work in the school. And although it has continued for many years, it is obvious that it may not be so easy in the future. So long as the vice-principal wishes us to be instruments of his own instructions and opinions only, it will be impossible to educate.

Yet is not the purpose of education to give power to the growing individual through experience and knowledge? Is not the idea, if not the practice, of education to give people intelligent control over their own lives? Do people have control over their own lives if they are not educated? How may they be educated if they are indoctrinated rather than asked to consider issues for themselves? Under the respectable disguises of loving, caring, providing for and protecting, the disreputable practice of securing the continuation of our own mistakes through future generations goes on.

But there are other ways of relating, as many hundreds of pupils I have taught over the years have shown me, and it is not only pupils who have done this. I have learned from some excellent teachers who have shown themselves prepared to relate to pupils as people, as developing adults, rather than as a race apart. And in one particular session it was the efforts and skill of a staff member which got me out of a frightening situation.

The school was an Inner London comprehensive and I had

before me twenty-four pupils from two separate groups. Our first sessions had gone remarkably well with the two form teachers sitting in. They explained that considering their presence, which they thought might be inhibiting, and the fact that there were four or five disruptive characters in the group, they were delighted with the response of the pupils. They suggested that they stay out for the remaining sessions now that I knew the group. So on the second week, I had the 14- to 15-year-olds to myself.

We were in a science lab (I'm not sure why) and within minutes of the session beginning I was in bad trouble. Without the presence of teachers, the four or five 'disruptive characters' gathered their two or three collaborators round them and decided to go it alone. A group of girls to the right of me were gathered round their leader, who was ostentatiously combing her hair, with her back to me, holding a mirror up as she did so. When I went over to her — all my calling having fallen on determined backs — and gently put my hand on her shoulder to gain her attention, her friend spun round and practically spat at me: 'That is an assault. Get your hands off her.'

I replied, something along the lines of: 'The four of you have been colluding in wilful neglect. How do you expect a teacher to conduct a lesson when you appear determined to prevent the course of education?'

In the meantime another one of the 'characters', a boy, had gathered his coterie round him near the back of the class and was about to have a water-fight. Meanwhile a boy slumped near the front of the class was saying: 'I'm bored. When are we going to learn anything?'

Unfortunately, I had been on the verge of losing my voice as I entered the classroom, and could only speak quietly. I seldom raise my voice, but this was obviously an occasion which needed it, and I couldn't. So I went up to the boy who was bored and asked him if he would go and get the form teacher for me. He left the classroom — and didn't return.

Seeing him leave, a few others decided they would do the same and started strolling towards the door. I beat them to it, and asked them where they were going.

'Out,' said one boy.

'Do you usually wander out in the middle of a lesson?' I asked.

He shrugged and stood where he was. It was one of the many occasions in a classroom when I have been glad of my height for there is no doubt that height is an asset, especially in an emergency. Since he wasn't going to go away, and others were close behind him, I decided to stay where I was, barring the exit, and to talk from there. But there were other diversions going on. A group of four or five boys were practically coming to blows over a cube which one of them had. He refused to give it to me. So, carefully, without touching him, I got hold of the part of it not covered by his hand and slowly, for he was fighting me every centimetre of the way, pulled it away from him. Obviously it was a battle of wills and I could not afford to lose.

It was not, as I understood it, his, and I put it in my bag saying that the person who owned it would have it back at the end of the session. That person came up to me every five or ten minutes and asked for it back, in a determinedly exasperating way. I asked the people who were prepared to learn — there were about ten of them it seemed — to bring their chairs round the door, and from then until the end of the hour-long session I worked with them with frequent interruptions as someone tried to demolish a venetian blind or start a water-fight again. At last, the form teacher came back, five minutes before the end of the session, to find me 'holding the fort' in that manner.

I was very frightened. I did not know how I would cope if any of the pupils had physically accosted me. It was a school where I had seen a female member of staff pushed aside by a boy the year before so that she almost fell down a flight of stairs. And obviously I was alarmed that I was doing such a lousy job in a classroom. What did this say about my abilities as a teacher? Should I not retire and find a job that I wasn't quite so bad at?

The form teacher was very surprised at what he saw — and visibly furious. With the benefit of knowing the pupils he was able to *be* angry. He told them what he thought of them and publicly apologized to me. By that time I had gathered enough breathing space and felt I too had an apology to make. I told them I wanted to apologize to all the people in the classroom who wanted to learn for not having provided them with the circumstances to do so. Then I requested that the people who were disrupting this session to say why they had done so and to let me know what I could have done to make things better. I ended miserably 'As far as I am concerned, I have failed today as a teacher, and it's not a very pleasant feeling to walk away with.'

The group then spoke out hotly, and started wrangling among themselves.

'You're not a failure, Miss: it's them, acting stupid all the time.'

'You're the one who's acting stupid, not me.'

And it went on like that for a few minutes until the form master called a halt, for it was the end of the school day, and he and I had a talk.

'Do you want to come back next week?' he asked. 'I wouldn't blame you if you didn't.'

'I think it's important that I do,' I said, 'but I'd like to come early to see what their responses have been.'

The following week, the form teacher was smiling and relaxed.

'That session last week has really set off a reaction,' he said. 'We've had some marvellous stuff from them, and it's been really beneficial. We had a big talk about what happened, and they've been arguing it out among themselves too. Basically, the people who are disrupting lessons have been put on the spot because a lot of the kids felt very protective towards you. One of the comments was: "Well, do you want teachers who are going to shout at us all the time. When she tries to be okay and nice to you you create trouble. You're always complaining teachers are bossy and push you around, and what do you do when you're treated like a human being?"

'We found it most rewarding because we've really discussed an awful lot about feelings and attitudes and taking liberties, and while it was rough for you, it's certainly been worthwhile for us.'

I had intended to have a discussion that week about what had happened, but decided, since it had already been so much talked about, not to. Instead I explained to the class that there was much material to get through, but that if, at the end of the session, anyone wanted to discuss what had happened the previous week, I would be happy to do so. In the presence of their form teacher, the session went well. There were cheery, in fact, affectionate goodbyes at the end of it.

I suppose you can never be quite sure exactly what you learn from a bad experience, but there were a number of points raised by this lesson, which incidentally, happened after I had been teaching for five years. I am unlikely to be persuaded ever again to take a session in a laboratory — unless a member of staff is present. It is rather a lot to ask a stranger in a school to cope with twenty-four pupils, let alone a couple of dozen bunsen burners and taps as well. Although most of the sessions I take are not attended by a staff member, I will nevertheless ask for one to be present if there are as many as four or five disruptive pupils in a group. It is a great handicap not to know the names of the pupils. And when you are taking as many as three different groups of twenty people in a week, it is impossible to remember names, even — and this happens only rarely — when you are given a list of them.

A classroom session like this, taken out of context, seems to support the horror stories of how 'they will run wild if you let them'. People will give you graphic details, even from primary schools, of occasions when this has happened, ending up with the moral that you have to tame them as you would young lions, and 'make sure they know where they are with you'. In a cage? I remember particularly a chilling account of a young teacher's experience with 5-year-olds. The trouble had begun with a boy who kept on turning round (the children were seated in uniform rows) and messing up the paints of the boy behind him. The teacher asked him a number of times to stop and he would not. She began to get exasperated, and confessed she wanted to hit him, but knew she mustn't. Her voice became sharper. Some of the other children began to get restive and fretful, so she said they could have some time away from their desks in the play area in a corner of the classroom. She sat down for a moment, as they practically stampeded from their seats, and said she was shaking with barely-contained anger.

Within a minute she had a scene on her hands which she says she will never forget: 'They were behaving like animals. I couldn't move. I felt as if I was hypnotised by what was going on. They totally destroyed the wendy house. Some of them were screaming and they were wading in to destroy everything in sight. Then a few of the girls started crying, and I got up. I felt very weak. They had spent themselves.'

This person gave up teaching a few years later. I sat in on a few of her classes as a student teacher myself and can only describe her as a strict disciplinarian. Yes, she was kind, but in a patronizing, objective way. She called them 'dear children' and, to my embarrassment, made them chant 'Good morning, Miss Lee' in unison every morning I came in. I clearly remember thinking that the children were like objects to her, like dolls, and she visibly withdrew from spontaneous contact with them. Yes, she would take a girl's hand and walk her to the wendy house; but she held the hand as if it were an object, and patted it before putting it down again. She needed to keep her distance from them and it was this which shaped her teaching. Since spontaneity is a particular characteristic and requirement of young children, her inability in this area, and her methodically controlled approach, must have made classroom life like an entrapment for her pupils. Yet her version of the story, told in the staffroom, served to support her fear that they needed to be 'watched like hawks' in case they became disruptive.

If we do believe that children and teenagers are, inherently, young savages needing to be brought into line then we *have* completely failed in any basic tending of our young. What changed these people from 'lovable' babies into monsters? And since teenagers are only a few years away from adulthood, is there a metamorphosis which changes a 15-year-old 'animal' into an 18-year-old human? Why are adults accepted as having rights (within society's accepted mores) to be the people they are, and why are teenagers not allowed these rights?

Perhaps the answer is to do with sexuality — and respect. Since sexual development is so prominent a part of adolescence, and since we fear this sexual development may lead to 'premature' sexual activity, perhaps we 'clamp down' on teenagers because of this. And is not 'clamping down' or repressing disrespectful? Was it the intrinsic 'disruptiveness' of her pupils which made the primary school teacher say she had to 'watch them like hawks', or was their behaviour caused by her lack of consideration of their specific needs — in other words, her lack of respect for them? Can we accommodate adolescence respectfully, or do we have to be repressive for fear of early sexual activity? And if we are repressive, how may young people grow up with true healthy respect for themselves and others?

This phrase, 'healthy respect', is in itself an illustration of our problems and confusions. Yes, true respect is healthy, and yet the phrase is normally used idiomatically in a rather different way. To have a 'healthy respect' for someone means to fear them. You don't necessarily *respect* someone for whom you have 'healthy respect' but you do as they say for fear of retribution. In the classroom, according young people respect and taking pains to let them know you do not wish to display yourself as superior to them is, I believe, a necessary antidote to the lack or respect they, and in fact most of us, receive elsewhere. And surprising discoveries result from this: like the time, in a class of 14-year-old so-called monsters, when I unintentionally uncovered a sympathy we do not usually associate with teenagers.

I had thought this group did not want to learn because they were being giggly and restless. After about five minutes of this, more in despair than a spirit of enquiry I said: 'Will you please do me a favour and tell me what's up. I'd be better off in a dole queue than trying to teach you lot at the moment.'

One of the boys came to my assistance by pointing to the limp, bedraggled demonstration sheath sticking out of the side of the bag I had put down by the side of my desk which contained the contraceptives I was going to show them after the morning break. Another of the boys said 'You shouldn't have told her, you berk.'

Another person said 'Well she *did* ask, didn't she?'

The first boy said 'But you didn't have to tell her.'

I agreed with him and asked the class generally if they thought I should have been told and if so why. One girl came up with the offering: 'We felt sorry for you, Miss. We didn't want you to end up on the dole queue.'

That lesson ended by being a discussion on kindness and I realized I was struck by their kindness because it must have been something I thought was unusual. In other words, I must have had tucked away in my mind somewhere the thought that teenagers are unkind. As adults, as teachers, we do not want to be considered but obeyed. To present ourselves as vulnerable means we would lose our power and we are not prepared to do this, though I believe we should find our pupils kinder than we think if we took them into our confidence.

I cannot accept that young people are not given respect because they do not, by definition, deserve it. I believe we subconsciously define them as unworthy of respect. When there is talk about young people running wild through lack of discipline, my private view is that they are running wild for lack of respect.

It is a fertile subject in the classroom. You could spend a whole weekful of lessons, let alone one out of a limited number, discussing the subject of respect. Where do feelings of self-esteem come from? What is the difference between the respect other people give you and the respect you have for yourself? How do you show respect for people? Is it possible to like someone and not respect them? Is it possible to love someone and not respect them? Does being unemployed make you lose respect for yourself. Should it?

Another interesting aspect is to look at the phrase: 'respecting a girl'. The boys will tell you that 'respecting a girl' means *not* making love with her. Yet adults who respect *do* make love. For couples who are used to lovemaking one partner would feel rejected if the other withheld sexual intimacy without there being a good reason for it. So how may a boy develop from a person with the feeling that making love is not respectful into a man with the understanding that it is? And here a further aspect of respect emerges, for if the boy 'respects' the law as it at present stands, he will not make love with a girl who is younger than sixteen.

The rewards from having an open discussion of this sort are immense. I clearly remember a group of 14-year-olds in an all-girls school. With the group numbering only eight, we had some of the best sessions in which I have ever been involved.

At the end of the one double lesson the girls did not want me to leave, but because the bell had brought them back to the constrictions of what life is usually like, they were unable at first to ask me to stay. Instead, one of them said hesitantly: 'I suppose you're going for coffee now, Miss. . . .' What she was really saying was clear and I answered: 'Not necessarily.' The other girls then asked me to stay and talk to them during break and I said I would be very happy to do so. 'But you'll be missing your coffee, Miss,' said the original girl. I replied I would prefer to stay and talk with them than drink coffee. They were so surprised that an adult would prefer their company that they could hardly believe it.

When I chose to stay I realized I had given them a sense of their own worth that was rare for them. They had been used to the idea of adults not enjoying their company. Given an opportunity to be the lovable young women they were for an hour or two, was an insight into themselves which I hope will stay with them. There is a sense of delight and reverence you feel when young people forget the constraints placed upon them and become absorbed in the excitement of learning. They forget the conditioning of school and home. They forget that you are a teacher and, instead of being inhibited, they begin to involve you in the thoughts and feelings that preoccupy them, and you begin to learn from one another.

My understanding of learning is above all that it is a respectful process. The activity of learning for oneself is an act of self-respect or fulfillment, and the activity of facilitating learning for others entails respecting them. To do this together is to have a respectful and fulfilling relationship. But this learning can only take place if the pupils' entitlement to talk with me is as important as my right to talk with them. If we basically view teenagers as an alien species, as 'animals to be tamed', or as sexual beings to be curbed, we withhold from them this right.

5 The Moral Monopoly

I HAVE met a number of people who have set themselves up as guardians of public decency and they have all dismayed me. One person I remember in particular was a Harley Street specialist I interviewed about a matter relating to public health and safety who had a need to tell me how he thought all criminals should be castrated. We were not talking about criminals or castration and I found the eagerness with which he brought our interview round to this topic perturbing.

Why castration? What was so especially effective about such an extreme form of punishment was, he thought, that 'people's criminal urges are tied up with sex. That's why you get less women committing crimes; they're not so sexually aggressive. They never had any trouble with eunuchs being violent. It's been well known for countless centuries that if you castrate a man he becomes peaceable. It's just that we're too soft in this country to do it.'

His opinion was apparently unalterable. He is a man who firmly believes in his own ability to be right and in his ability to 'do good' for the country. He sits on a number of committees, I only hope with people who do not share his extraordinary views. So fervent was he in advocating castration that he was prepared to go into print stating his opinions on the subject. I was not. But the idea that sex and criminality go together is, I am afraid, not uncommon. We believe we have come some way towards sexual enlightenment—too far for many—but in fact sex as something free from prejudice has not, for the vast majority, arrived yet.

That probably seems a ludicrous statement to make in the light of the sort of society we live in where sex on television, sex in Soho, sex on chat-shows and sex in magazines would all seem to prove, if anything, that there is too much emphasis on sex. So perhaps it is worth looking at the 'sex' that is around to see what it is really all about. You do not have to look far for an answer — it is about money. If you accept that *real sex* is the most intimate way known to us of showing our love for one another, if you accept that it is about affection, mutual enjoyment, fulfillment and trust, then you would have to conclude that there is no sex in Soho. But there is money. People pay large sums of money either out of curiosity, need, or boredom, to have displayed for them films and 'live' shows which parody sex. I am astounded that people still take this as a sign of our sexual enlightenment, that they believe Soho indicates our permissiveness. If we were really sexually liberated, Soho would not be able to function, let alone make money, except perhaps as a farce. Soho exploits people's sexual weaknesses, and society and the schools perpetuate those weaknesses, though the opportunity is there to do otherwise.

I have a theory that if we really were living in a society which accepted sex, Soho would be out of business. If we were sexually enlightened, the owners of the places I have looked at would be had up under the Trade Descriptions act for not providing anything, either visually or spiritually which approximates to a sexual good time. But as it is, Soho's barren wares are actually mistaken for the real thing, otherwise why else would we call them an example of sexual licence? My own criticism of Soho is not that it is an area of heaving sexuality, but that it is not.

It is the money that is made out of sex, the way it has been taken up and commercialized, not to give us pleasure but to make us buy commodities, which makes us believe sex is all around. And if there is money to be made out of exploiting something it is a sign that there is a weakness there to be exploited. If we all lived on a South Sea Islands Paradise and accepted nakedness, it is obvious that page three of *The Sun* would not sell too well. As it is, the picture of a near-naked female on page three has made the newspaper's proprietor a lot of money, not because we are too sexy as a nation, but because we are too inhibited.

The picture on page three often comes to school with me, partly because she is so familiar it makes a good starting point.

A session begins with my holding up the latest topless daily dolly, and asking the class who she is.

They don't know.
'*What* is it?' I ask.
'A woman's body,' says one boy, and to all round laughter: 'Anyone can see that.'
'So it's a woman's body and not a woman,' I say.
'Well, it's a woman too.'

'But do you ever remember her name?'

'No, Miss,' says the same boy, and to further laughter: 'But I'd certainly remember her tits!'

'What is the difference between a subject and an object?' I ask.

Baffled silence.

'Is this woman a subject or an object?'

'Both,' says one of the boys, but the girls are beginning to pick up the point behind the questions and one of them says: 'An object Miss, because her name doesn't matter.'

'Is this picture in any way worrying?' I ask.

The boys shrug and think not, but again one of the girls says: 'It makes women cheap, Miss.'

'How does it do that?'

They are not quite sure. One of the boys ventures: 'Because it makes them objects to be gawped at.'

'Does it matter if women are made into objects?'

Silence.

'Come on. Do you treat women as objects or as people, and what is the difference?'

Silence.

'Am I an object or a person?'

'A person, Miss'

'What is the difference between the way you would treat me as a person and the way you would treat me as an object?'

Silence.

'Isn't it something to do with relationship. Don't you have a relationship with a person in a way you don't with an object? I am a person, a football is an object. What is the difference between the way you treat a football and the way you treat a person?'

We begin to work out the differences. Obviously you kick a football around, and use it for a specific purpose after which, generally speaking, you push it aside until you want to use it again. The object is in your *control*. It doesn't answer back. It is possible to be violent towards an object with no comebacks. You can kick a stone in the street. Are you more likely to be violent towards a person if you treat them as an object? Slowly, step by step, they work their way towards the idea of sex objects, and the time is right for a short rôle-play session on pin-up girls.

After a bit of discussion we find three people. One is a serious girl, quite capable of standing her ground and of taking no nonsense from any of the boys. The other is a girl with a more extrovert personality. She enjoys laughing, but is also well equipped to take care of herself. Choosing the boy is more difficult. Eventually one chooses himself as having what it takes — the ability to chat easily and to stay out of trouble. The scene is a small party. The two girls are both there, one is a page three girl from a picture in *The Sun* the day before, the other is, at her own request, a student. The two girls are sitting on chairs. The boy is asked to enter the room and speak to either of them for whatever reason he chooses. He breezes up to the page three girl.

'Saw you in the papers yesterday,' he says with ill-concealed expectation.

'Oh yes,' she says dismissively turning her head away.

'You've got a great body,' he says 'It was a smashing picture.'

'Glad you think so,' she replies.

'Do you fancy . . .?' he doesn't finish partly because both the girl and the rest of the class erupt in laughter. He confirms his question was to ask her to have sex with him.

'Okay,' I say. 'You've made a beeline for this lady. Now try talking with the other one.'

This time his approach is completely different. His is not jauntily confident, and has to stand in the corner for a moment to work out his approach. It is:

'I haven't seen you here before.'

'No,' says the girl primly.

Awkward silence. Then *she* says:

'I'm a friend of David's. Are you?'

'Yes,' he says in a relieved manner, 'I've known David for years. We play football together.'

'Do you like playing football?' she asks.

'Yes, I play quite a lot.'

'Do you play near here?' she asks.

'Yes, sometimes we play over at the Marshes. It depends if me dad can give me a lift over.'

Awkward silence. Awkward silence continues.

'The music's good isn't it,' he says.

'Yes,' she says. No more conversation ensues.

The differences between object and person are then easier to discuss. The boy sees that with the first girl he is doing all the running because of an assumption he has made about her — that she will go to bed. Why has he made the assumption? He agrees it is because she has had her picture 'splashed across' the papers. With the second girl he is not confident for he doesn't know how she's going to react.

'You aren't by any chance considering her feelings?' I ask mischievously. . . .

It all seems a far cry from sex and violence, but it is not, for it is obvious that teenagers form an automatic link between the two, without questioning it. They accept it as they accept, say, the link between smoking and lung cancer. With boys, in particular, it is evident that much of their sexual thinking is aggressive. Phrases like: 'Give her one' are used for sexual intercourse.

I once took a session with a group of young men of sixteen to eighteen (in an Intermediate Treatment Centre not a school) where the aggression was barely containable. After they had turned down all of the topics I had suggested, I asked if there was any subject they would like to talk about.

'Blue movies.'

'Okay,' I say. 'What would you like to discuss about blue movies?'

'Women having it with dogs.'

'Yeah,' another boy says, 'My friend's got a video of a woman doing it with an alsation!'

They are obviously excited by this.

'Do you get turned on by that?' I ask quietly.

They stop, defensively.

'Nah, it's just a lark.'

'The way you were talking it seemed as if it was more than lark. Why does women doing it with dogs excite you?'

'You see 'er panting for it. An' the dogs riding 'er.'

'I tell you it's disgusting,' says one of the group with obvious relish.

'Is this anything to do with sex?' I ask.

'Course it is,' they reply.

'I don't think it is. It's not to do with sex at all. It's to do with only one thing – violence against women. You are excited by women doing it with dogs because you are excited by seeing women degraded. Enjoying seeing people being degraded is not sexual enjoyment — it's sadism.'

'But sadism is sex,' says one of them.

'It's perverted sex,' I say.

'Yeah, but lots of sex is about perversions.' Pause, and then loud laughter.

'We're all perverts here, ain't we?'

'That's like calling murder a relationship,' I reply. 'If I have murderous feelings towards you I will have a relationship with you that involves me murdering you. But you don't try and say that human relationships are about murder. Now don't try and tell me that sexual relationships are about sadism and perversion. . . . If that's what they are to you then you've got problems. . . .'

For the first time, the group is taking notice of me. I have been with them for about an hour by this time and the going is devastatingly rough. What can anybody do with a dozen young men in this state, to make sexual education mean anything. Do you give them a lecture on the dangers of VD: or steer clear of them and hope you never meet one of them on a dark night?

'You lot don't seem to know much about sex,' I venture.

Uncomfortable silence.

'Well, that's what you're here for. To teach us it all.'

They brighten up at this prospect, and get cheeky again.

They ask to see the contents of my bag. The bag has contraceptives in it. Since boys with their mechanistic outlook often like gadgets, talking about contraceptives is a good way of introducing them to the notion of female sexuality as opposed to sexual perversions. And except for the pill, female contraception is something they know practically nothing about. So we look at the contraceptives and they are, for the most part, attentive and interested.

At the end one boy leans back in his seat and says: 'Well, what would you say turns a woman on, then. I mean what gets her going?'

Now it might not seem the most profound, or even the most advised question in the world, but it is a long haul up from alsatian dogs. It does at least have an element in it of a desire to please rather than a need to offend.

But it is on account of sessions like this that detractors of sex education get 'up in arms'. It is disgusting that we are encouraging young men to discuss blue movies, it is disgusting that four-letter words are being used in classrooms and it is the reason why society is 'going to the dogs'. Yet it wasn't sex *education* which gave the young men in this group their outlook (and is it safe for them or for society that they have them?) and it wasn't I who 'taught' teenagers their words.

One young man in the group was so estranged from any 'real' idea of sex that throughout the session all his questions were directed to how he could avoid 'doing it' with a human, and they were not 'try-ons' or jokes.

He asked: 'Could you do it with a pillow?'

'I don't know,' I replied. 'Why would you want to do it with a pillow?'

Silence. Then a little later:

'Could you do it with a toilet roll?'

'It might be possible to "do it" with the inner cardboard tube of a toilet roll,' I replied, 'but you'd probably hurt yourself because the penis is sensitive and needs lubrication or a pliable soft surface in order to move without becoming sore.'

He replied: 'So what's wrong with a pillow?'

'What's wrong with a person?' I asked.

'Oh, 'e don't like people,' someone else replied.

Surely it is important that attitudes like these are aired and challenged rather than allowed to fester? Yet the upholders of public morals are disturbed by encounters like these and seek to use them to shock ordinary decent people by telling them how people like me are deforming the minds of young people by discussing blue movies; how people like me encourage young people to premature and unloving sex; how sex education should be taught only in a moral context, by people fit to teach the subject. If we take the question of morality; one of the problems with arguments about sex education and morality is that sex is singled out as the only area of education deserving moral scrutiny. What about history? On our understanding of history depends to a marked degree our knowledge of religion, our perspective of the world as it has developed and grown and our understanding of our present position. Yet the history lessons at the schools I attended were, I now think, educational travesties, dominated exclusively by ideas of national self-aggrandisement and imperialism. They glorified war and de-humanized black people. At very least, the lessons did not fit me for life in a multiracial society with a cold war crudely guarded by nuclear weapons. Is there any subject which should be taught without a moral context?

In any case, morality is not absent from any sex education class I have been in. Take the following example of a class of fifthformers. I asked the class if, for our last double lesson, there was a particular issue they would like to discuss or debate. A number of people said 'abortion,' so I asked them to come prepared to talk about this, explaining that it would not matter if they could not remember all the facts because what I was really interested in was their feelings and opinions on the subject. By this I hoped to include everyone in the class and not just the people who were high achievers. The following week I asked four people to give talks, two 'for' and two 'against' abortion.

The next hour-and-a-half was a revelation to me. The talks were excellent, and covered aspects of abortion that I had not thought of myself. One of the girls who spoke against abortion said the following: 'I don't think there should be abortion, even if you could tell there was doing to be a deformed child, because the world needs deformed children. . . .'

When asked why she said: 'Deformed children make us behave better than we normally do and they bring out things in us which wouldn't be brought out otherwise. They make us care for them in a special way and give them extra love, and we wouldn't do this with ordinary people.'

I was fascinated by this reply and we all had a long discussion about it. Why did she think we were incapable of giving extra love to people who were not deformed? Were there not many living people who were deformed by car accidents, crippled with pain from long illnesses, and what about mental and emotional pain? Did we have much concern or love for people whose parents die or who lose a close friend? She said that she thought it was easier to love babies because they were helpless and much more difficult to love crippled adults.

So then we asked her: 'What about the deformed babies who grow up into deformed adults? Isn't it cruel "deliberately" to bring deformed babies into the world knowing they will have progressively less love as they grow older? Why do we love adults less?'

I then asked the question: 'Is it fair to work out whether or not you allow a deformed child to be born from our own needs — whether or not it is better for us? Isn't it callous, and a terrible comment upon our progress as human beings to say that we want a deformed child to be born just to show us how to love well?'

We had many conflicting opinions at this stage. One boy said: 'But we have to have something to compare ourselves with, Miss, otherwise how would we know when we're well off?'

I asked if he needed to know children were starving elsewhere in order to enjoy his food, but I could see what he meant, and we had a discussion about comparisons and competitiveness. Was it right that we should have to have people worse off than ourselves in order for us to feel better off? What sort of attitude did that mean we had towards others, and towards ourselves? What about the people who were worse off all the time? Did we think it was fair that some people should be condemned to a worse-off life? Were there any other ways of judging the quality of our lives besides comparing them with the lives of others? One boy said: 'Feeling good in yourself, Miss.'

Not only was I delighted with this reply, but doubly pleased that it came from the person it did. I had noticed this particular boy had been quiet for the previous weeks. I remember thinking that, while he seemed interested, he was at the same time ill at ease and until now had said nothing at all. We then began to discuss how you felt good within yourself, by what means, through what feelings or actions and whether there was a conflict between feeling good within ourselves and feeling good within society. How many decisions are made for ourselves and how many have to take into account the wishes and needs of other people?

We eventually returned to the topic of abortion. If we believed that abortion was wrong did we believe that of all abortion? They thought that cases where the mother's or the baby's life was endangered were cases where abortion should be allowed. And, throughout these talks, the complexity of morality was becoming clearer to them. Is it immoral to take a growing foetus from the womb or is it immoral to bring an unwanted child into the world? How do we judge morality? What is it? Who decides it? What governs it?

I teach this way because I believe this kind of open-ended discussion is infinitely more valuable than dogmatizing about morality. Completely the opposite view is put by a booklet called, deceptively, *Sound Sex Education*, which was produced by the Order of Christian Unity. In their view teachers like myself should be banned from classrooms.

The booklet has an introduction by Sir John Peel, former Surgeon Gynaecologist to the Queen, in which he welcomes the publication as a valuable contribution to the debate on sex education. This misnamed publication is couched in right and sane phrases and it is all the more unfortunate, therefore, that it studiously ignores the position and feelings of the adolescents it is supposed to be providing for, whose sexuality is treated as something nasty to be overcome rather than a reality to be looked at.

Masturbation, for example, is described in the following terms: 'Some boys' [information tells us it is the majority, not some] 'may get into the habit of masturbating – even unconsciously — when very young. This is an addictive, introspective practice, so the more you do this the harder it is to stop. This means that the sooner you can achieve the "self-control" we have mentioned the better it will be for you.'

This booklet has found its way into dozens of schools in Britain, and the chairman of the Order, Lady Watherston, makes no secret of the fact that they are hoping to get this and a future document into all schools, through the backing of the Education Minister from whom she was confident of strong support and encouragement. It is selling steadily, at about the rate of a thousand copies a year, and is being promoted in schools round the country. An Irish edition is due to be published and also an American version.

Sound Sex Education is a demonstration of the morals of its authors. There are many references to morality, all of which make the implicit, and sometimes explicit, statement that the form of morality decided upon by the authors is the only right form. It argues against sex education being taught within 'a moral vacuum', something I would agree with. The problem is that their definition of 'moral vacuum' comes close to my definition of teaching. The authors of this document on sex education leave you in no doubt that children are to be indoctrinated with all that the writers think is sound and right. Personally I consider that in itself, to be immoral, for it is denying individuals the right to develop critical faculties by which they can come to make their own decisions.

The notion that it is essential for young people to be 'told' the difference between right and wrong in a dogmatic way presents you with many contradictions. In the case of abortion, the law itself has changed several times in recent years. The question, therefore, of whether abortion is 'right' or 'wrong' is surely best dealt with by permitting young people the fullest possible information on the subject and allowing them to judge for themselves.

In the debate as to whether sex educators like myself encourage young people to premature and unloving sex, it should be considered what kind of ideas about sex young people already have. I often ask young people how much sex education they have received, and the answers are salutary. One 15-year-old girl told a colleague: 'In biology they taught us about rats, but honestly, Miss, I wouldn't want to do it with a rat. . . .'

Well over 80 per cent of the roughly 1,500 teenagers I have seen in eight years of teaching say they have had no sex education whatsoever at home. No member of their family has explained to them how sexual intercourse takes place, how a baby is born or why sexual intercourse takes place. And the more you break down the questions asking for instance if they received sex education which they considered appropriate to the realities of their lives only a smattering respond positively.

Less than 20 teenagers out of a figure of 1,500 felt they had been given any meaningful sex education and it was nearly always possible, beforehand, to tell who they were. They are conspicuous by their maturity and composure, and I do not think this is accidental or coincidental. I think it is because they have been helped through the maelstrom of sexual confusion in a positive way and are therefore less beset by anxieties and less accosted by spurious rumours than are their peers.

When I was a child there was a spate of war films showing on television, many of which were to do with torture. They illustrated the heroism of British soldiers under the direst of conditions. I do not know any 9-year-olds who were banished from living rooms as men were submitted to the most ghastly forms of sadism; yet the tut-tutting that went on when a kissing scene came on the screen was quite a disturbance with comments like: 'Why do they put this filth on?' The point I am making is an obvious one. What on earth are we thinking of when we do not trouble about children seeing films of people damaging each other in the most hideous ways, and yet are troubled about them watching scenes of people embracing with all their clothes on? And where are our senses if we believe one (the violence) will not affect children, and the other (an embrace) will seduce them? Either television does affect us or it does not. We cannot say violence on TV will not harm children and that pictures of couples kissing will, unless of course we think that violence does not damage the fibre of the nation and that affection does.

Another example of this anomaly relates to the way we treat teenage boys. Very few boys I have spoken with are cuddled by their parents. Yet two young men may get into a ring, designed especially for the purpose, and hit each other — occasionally with fatal consequences — in the name of a recognized sport called boxing. This activity is watched and taken up by young men. Yet if you showed a film of a couple in a ring making love it would be considered obscene and unfit for young people to see.

There is now an active anti-violence lobby in action, but it is interesting that where sex and violence meet — in rape for example — very little progress has been made in making the media act responsibly in what it depicts. I was at the initial meeting in London in March 1982 of a group of journalists and other people, like the women from the Rape Crisis Centres, who want to see rape represented by the media in a more responsible manner. One of the women from the Birmingham Rape Crisis Centre had kept a dossier of the press coverage of rape in national newspapers and magazines. It was obvious from look-ing at these cuttings that rape has a highly titillating value for much of the popular press, and that even the so-called serious press often fall far short of a fair presentation of rape. The women from Birmingham had also collated figures to show how rape cases attract a disproportionate amount of space in the popular press, compared with other, more common, serious offences. Rape is good copy.

By the time young people are old enough to be taking an interest in newspapers, sex and violence have been linked in their minds in such a way that not only are they spoken of in the same breath, but in such a way that sex is actually seen as the cause of violence. Rape is seen as a sexual act *per se* and a further sign of the dangers of there being too much 'sexual freedom', rather than as an intrinsic action of violence, as a need to dominate and defile a woman which takes a sexual form. It is easy from here, to make sex the culprit and let the real culprit — violence — go unattended to. It is not surprising therefore, that sex is believed to be a threat to the moral fibre of the nation. But is it? Is learning to be tender, to be considerate, to appreciate what it is like to feel real pleasure as opposed to the skin-flicks of alleged pleasure (like amusement arcades and junk films) bad for people?

It seems we think it is. Agencies like the Family Planning Association and the Brook Advisory Centres, which give teenagers contraceptive and many other kinds of advice are blamed for encouraging young people to have sex. But the figures speak for themselves. Dr Fay Hutchinson, medical officer of the Brook Advisory Centres in London says: 'Of the contraceptives we give, only one per cent are prescribed for girls under sixteen, most of whom are already sexually active. We are hardly encouraging girls under the Age of Consent to sexual activity when they are already sexually active before they come to us. But we *are* trying to prevent these girls from getting pregnant. Would people prefer we didn't?'

For my own part in the classroom I do not believe that sex education encourages sexual intercourse, but rather that, in the short term, it discourages it. I base this comment on observations of young people. I noticed soon after beginning sex education that young girls, who are the main recipients of contraceptive advice in the classroom (since there is only one contraceptive for men), were not overjoyed to be given it. I do not have an eager crowd of girls waiting to hear how they could have intercourse and not get pregnant. On the contrary, I find that young people have basically romantic and unrealistic ideas about sex, in which contraception does not feature. I noticed this as I moved from one school to another: girls still have the feeling that sex is something they do not have to think about because it is not for them to worry about it. They still believe in the romantic notion that one day sex will come into their lives and alter them in some pleasant, but spontaneous way.

If this does not fit into your idea of what modern teenage girls think about sex, it is because these feelings are ones that girls do a great deal to disguise. You discover them from stray comments and bits of information given over many weeks. In discussing relationships the vast majority of girls will still tell you that it is up to the boys to instigate friendships with a girl and they still consider it 'cheap' for girls to 'chat up' boys. Very few girls will tell you that there is nothing wrong with a girl talking to a boy. The girls also think of feelings associated with sex as being 'special feelings' reserved for sex only, which only become apparent when they start having sex. In other words, once sex begins, a special feeling attendant on it will also suddenly 'arrive'. They do not think of sexual intercourse as using feelings they have in any case — tenderness, warmth, compassion, friendliness, humour, fear. The bits and pieces have changed, but the essence has not: the 'riding off into the sunset happy ever after' syndrome is still around, only differently cloaked.

For the girls who have these notions, a discussion of the practical and necessary use of contraceptives is not an invitation to intercourse. It is far more likely to make them vow, as some of them do, not to be involved in sex ever. An invitation to young people to think about sex is not an invitation for them to do it, but rather the opposite. Sexuality is a complex issue for young people and recognizing just how complex is, if anything, a deterrent. In certain circumstances it is easy for them to stick their heads in the sand and let their bodies carry them away and then still not feel responsible for their actions when all the fuss starts. It is much more difficult to make a decision to engage in sex when you know what all the issues are. And if you do know what the issues are, and decide to go ahead in a responsible manner, it is not because sex education has perverted you but because it has enabled you to make up your own mind.

To the majority of young people who are still a long way off making up their own minds, it is initially perplexing and worrying, not alluring, to be faced with the issues surrounding sex generally, and teenage sex in particular. It is worrying to be faced with the thought that no contraceptive is 100 per cent safe; that society is very much against your having sex; that the girls risk, as they will tell you, getting themselves a bad name with the boys for sleeping around; that VD is a common infection among young people, and that some schools expel girls if they get pregnant. If you are asked to consider the consequences of young sex—pregnancy since young girls are highly fertile, and a possible law suit if the girl is under sixteen—you are not encouraged into sexual activity. Most young girls with a ro-manticized notion of their first sexual experience believe that somebody, somewhere, will make it all right on the night. I invite them to the idea that the only person who can make it all right for them, at any time, is themselves.

Encouraging people to their own authority also encourages them to responsibility. For most young people this is an alarm-ing prospect. I cannot place a 'thou shalt not' order on the blackboard in the vain hope of preventing some young people becoming sexually active, because that would be violating the principles of education as I see it. No series of lessons in which respect has played a fundamental part can end up with my issuing an order as to how people must behave. This is the reason that the few people who are ready to have sex at an early age do not find a message at the end of a lesson which says: NO SEXUAL INTERCOURSE. It is because this order is not issued that many people argue with sex education, but since ordering and education are incompatible you cannot on the one hand claim to be bringing young people to an awareness of their own authority and then, on the other, forbid them to use it.

6 An Agonized Aunty

IN PARENTS' meetings, in schools, and even among colleagues, I see all the time how deeply entrenched are our ideas that sex is basically unwholesome. I also had first-hand experience of this when I was writing what is currently called an 'agony' column for teenagers in a Fleet Street daily newspaper. In having to evaluate what could and could not be said in print I was sometimes left with the feeling that there was not one sexually enlightened adult who read it. At one time I was receiving more letters from parents telling me to use my position to 'bring their kids into line' than I was from young people needing help.

One confrontation in particular between the editor and myself during the course of that job, remains with me still. The matter of the argument was not to his liking, but then neither was it to mine. It concerned masturbation. I had received a number of letters from young boys asking if they would ruin their chances of having a normal sex life if they continued masturbating. These letters had come in over the months and most of them did not have return addresses so I could not write back to them privately. I was very concerned that I was letting these people down. I knew that the myth that masturbation makes you impotent was prevalent from the numbers of boys who asked me this either during or after a lesson. Because I could not reply personally to the letters it made it doubly important that the problem be dealt with in print. You may ask why the boys did not put their addresses to their names. This was not uncommon among the mail I received; about 50 per cent was from people who did not leave an address. When parents stop opening their children's letters, then children will feel safer letting you know where they live.

So I decided to write about masturbation in my column and explain the myths that still surround the subject. If it should seem rather an obvious solution to the problem, let me say that I had been trying to get the word 'masturbation' into the column for four weeks before I went into the editor's office, and had failed. The first time it went in — as a lead letter — I was asked to rewrite the column since masturbation was not a suitable subject for discussion. I argued that I was, after all, running a service for people and could hardly not deal with the problems to which they wanted to know the answer. But arguing seemed to be no use, so I compromised and put the letter at the bottom of the column rather than the top. It was cut out. For three weeks I kept on putting it back in and for three weeks they cut it out, so I went to the editor.

My argument was simple. I understood the paper did not like using the word, 'masturbation' but I had a duty to the young people I taught and helped. Did the editor realize he was, as far as I was concerned, condemning the young boys who had written to me to even more anxiety by refusing to allow me to answer their simple query? The editor was adamant: the subject of masturbation was not going to be dealt with in his 'family newspaper'.

'But,' I protested, 'I can show you sentences from this paper every week which talk about sexual activity, some of it in salacious and spectacular terms. Why, if you will print that, will you not print a letter about masturbation?'

He was adamant. He would not, and there, I am afraid, the matter ended. He tried to excuse himself on the grounds that: 'after all, masturbation is rather an ordinary topic. Don't you have more interesting letters than that to use?'

I asked him why he devoted so many stories every day to football when that was also 'ordinary' or to cookery columns, but I knew I was not, in the end, going to win. For a while I carried on so far as the censorship would allow but with a sense of regret. It has always bothered me that the writers of those letters waited in vain for a reply. I am sorry that we live in a society where values are such that the word 'masturbation' could not be used in the columns of a paper, yet where phrases like 'sex orgies' and 'teenage crime soars' are considered to be useable, no doubt 'in the public interest'.

Other adult objections to the letters and answers in my column were even more hardhitting. I realized that any signs of being 'soft' on the younger generation were frequently greeted angrily by adults who wrote in suggesting among other things that I should be sacked for giving such liberal advice. Lest you imagine the advice *was* liberal, one of the most vitriolic came after I had suggested that an 18-year-old boy take his crippled mother to the pub for a night out. He had written me a sweet letter explaining that he lived with his crippled mother and (what I took to be) his martyr of a father. In the name of caring for his wife singlehanded the boy's father had refused all help in the house and took entirely upon himself the burden of looking after his wife — a full-time job in itself — doing the housework, cooking and earning a living too. Commendable on the surface, but it made for a miserable home. His wife was left on her own while he was out working, which meant life was lonely for her, and when he came home he was so busy organizing everything that he had no time to include or to chat with his son. I suggested a number of things to the boy, both in the column and in a personal letter I wrote to him. In the last paragraph of the column I said something like: 'That house of yours needs some light and laughter in it. It is bad enough for your mother to be crippled, let alone to live trapped and alone in a miserable home. If you cannot improve the atmosphere in the house then take her out [she was capable of travelling in a wheelchair]. Wheel her down to the local pub in the evening and get to know people.'

The editor was informed in a letter which resulted from that column that young people spent far too much time in pubs in any case, as no doubt did I, and 'why doesn't your paper save itself some money and sack people who contribute such trash to its pages.' The lady who wrote that letter cannot be dismissed as a crank for she was not alone in her condemnation. Whenever I mentioned anything to do with sex or contraception there would be a spate of letters from adults saying that 16- and 17-year-olds should not be given such information. I replied to these letters considerately on most occasions, although there was one letter which made me so angry that I did not. I had given some advice to a girl seeking a breast reduction operation. I had explained that because she was only sixteen she would not be able to have an operation immediately, and I gave her the name of a place to go to discuss her problem with somebody more qualified than I am to explain the medical aspects of it. I also said that I would send her privately the names of certain bras which had the effect of making you look smaller.

As a result of that column I received a long letter from a brigadier who was quivering with rage that I should be putting such filth in the papers. He said it was all perverted rubbish to try and titillate people and that it was made up in any case, otherwise why did I not print the names and addresses of people who wrote to me? I wrote back explaining that my column was designed to help young people with problems and that none of them wanted their names and addresses in print for everyone to see what was ailing them. I said that anyone who felt the column titillated them would have to look to themselves for the cause of the problem and not to me. I could not resist ending the letter with: 'Anyone who judges the use of the word, "breast" in the context of Saturday's column to be cause for apoplexy is, himself, perverted. Yours sincerely.'

However, the column was not all bad news. I began to enter into regular correspondence with one or two young people who obviously had a great deal to work through and, since I enjoy writing letters, it was a pleasure to be paid for the privilege. I learned a great deal from becoming accustomed to read between the lines, which is where most of the information given and help asked for lay, and some of the letters of thanks or appreciation which I received were all the more delightful for being so unexpected. I think I probably received about half a dozen hoax letters during the eighteen months I wrote the column: I say, 'think', because you can never be sure. One letter I felt sure was a hoax turned out not to be. It was from a girl of sixteen who was involved in such strange sexual practises that I felt sure her letter was not genuine. I replied as if it were because, as I say, you cannot be sure and it would be damaging if someone who was genuinely in trouble did not receive help. It turned out that this letter was genuine. I know, because I had advised her to go and see a particular youth agency which, at that time, helped young people with sexual problems. The social worker there called me about a month later to thank me for referring the girl to her. Her father had been having sexual intercourse with her since she was ten and she was in a highly disturbed state.

One of my favourite correspondents over those eighteen months was a boy whom, for the sake of anonymity I shall call John. John had been waiting for a service like mine to come on the market for some time. He was a professional seeker of help, even at the age of fifteen, and when I learned more about his background I understood why he made himself known to me almost as soon as my column began. His letter was formal — addressed to Miss Lee — and told of his love for a married woman nearly twice his age. He implored me not to tell him this was puppy love and said he was badly in need of help because he was going out of his mind through love of this lady. He concluded by letting me know that he had tried every other agony columnist in the business and that 'they'd been no help at all', so now he was coming to me to see if I could do any better. He was certainly letting me know what I was up against!

I wrote John a long personal letter — he had asked me not to put his problem in the paper. I put a lot of energy and inspiration into that letter. I explained how the difference between adulthood and teenage years is not the intensity with which you feel love, but in the amount of understanding of and control over your emotions which you have. I then went on to ask him a lot of questions feeling that this was a better way of learning more from him than passing comment.

Any fine feelings I had about that reply were soon knocked on the head. John's response to my letter let me know that I was in for a difficult time in the next few months. 'Thankyou for your letter,' he said. 'Your advice was no good at all. . . . However, I now have a different problem for you. . . .'

The second instalment of John's life-story seemed to be telling me more about what his real problems were, something which I do not think his first letter revealed. His 'new' problem was that he enjoyed dressing up in women's clothes. This explained why he should wish to baby-sit for a woman of twenty-eight. When she and her husband went out it would give him the time and opportunity to dress up in her clothes. At home he probably did not have the chance to do this and, in any case, his mother's clothes would be far less interesting. I still had a feeling there was a lot more to come, but I treated the new problem as I had done the first one, as an entity in itself. I wrote that I'd mentioned his problem to a friend and suggested John might like to speak to him personally.

I had in fact been talking with the director of another agency which helps young people and he had indeed said that there had been a spate of young people coming forward claiming to be transvestites. He was not sure why. Either these people had always been there and only now felt able to talk about it, or it was a new craze, perhaps occasioned by the way punk groups were dressing up. I rang this director and told him about John so that he and his staff would look out for him if he called. I, in the meantime, got a by-return-of-post reply from John which said: 'Thanks a ton. Have an appointment on Monday.'

Then all went quiet for a bit until two months later when another letter arrived. It was a tentative, shy communication which began: 'Dear Miss, you may remember me. I wrote to you a few months ago saying I was in love with a married women, and then I wrote saying I dressed up in women's clothes (I don't do that any more). Well, now I have a different problem for you. . . .'

John's different problem was his real one and, as I read it, I wished every adult in the country could read it too. It was a difficult, uncontrived, disjointed communication about what it is like to be a teenager growing up with practically no sense of your own identity in a busy and frightening world. He explained that he could not talk with his elderly mother; that his dad had died when he was young; how he could not get on with people of his own age. He was isolated from the world, a problem he shared with thousands of young people in London alone. The agencies with which I was in touch while writing my column were deluged with young people who did not know who they were, how to express themselves and what to do with themselves. They are the children of parents who have been too busy to talk with them, children who have been reared on a diet of television and comic strips. The sorts of problems with which they present you have been going on for fifteen years and they cannot be sorted out in a half-hour chat or even months of specialist care (presuming that this were available, which it is not).

But some help is, I believe, better than none, so I wrote another long letter to my young friend, John, in the hope that he might find something in it somewhere to give him some comfort or inspiration. I sent him the names of every appropriate teenage support group I could think of. I observed that I thought he had a lot going for him if he was prepared to begin going out and meeting the world rather than withdrawing from it, and, feeling quite depressed myself by this time, I sat back and waited.

All was quiet for a few months and then to my relief another letter in the by now familiar handwriting arrived. John was feeling a bit better and thanked me profusely for my previous letter. Life was improving, I think because he had now left school and had started a job. He explained that there were two girls where he worked and he wanted to take one of them out. But he didn't know how to ask a girl, and furthermore when he did take her out he did not know how to kiss her and he also wanted to know if he should kiss her the first time and if so where?[!]

My letter in return was, perforce, another long one. How do you cope with that lot and its implications in less than a book on 'how to conduct your own life when you've had no training?' I went into a long, rambling discourse on the nature and advisability of affectionate contact with other people. However, as I did not hear from John for such a long time after sending it off, I eventually dropped him a few lines saying I hoped he was okay and not to feel he had to have a problem in order to write to me: it would be nice to hear how he was getting along. I was concerned that John might want to remain in contact but would not know how to do so, and if he wanted to I was happy to continue hearing from him. It seemed he needed a friend, which I was glad to be, and I did not want him to return to the feeling of being completely alone in the world.

I was right in imagining that John wanted to remain in contact because I received another letter from him by return of post. It was a nice letter: he thanked me for my previous communication, and then came to the real explanation of his silence. 'I didn't need your advice about kissing,' he wrote. 'When I asked the first girl out she said "no" and when I asked the other one she said "no" too.'

It was obvious from the way he phrased the letter that the girls had been together when he had asked them out, and I had not been alert enough to pick up from his letter the fact that either of them would do! It seems from that as if it is going to be a long time before John is the sort of person who is capable of winning a female heart. I am still not sure he fully understands that asking two girls out in front of each other is not the best way to endear himself to either.

I still hear from John even though I stopped doing the column a number of years ago. For a while his letters were forwarded to me from the paper and I eventually gave him my home address. He has so many difficulties that I shudder to imagine what life must be, living inside John's skin. People like John have spent their whole lives being cheated of their birthright — their natural ability to become themselves — and a young person who has been inhabiting the sort of emotional desert which surrounds John does not change into a lively, well-balanced teenager overnight.

Young people become like John because they have not been given the right opportunities to grow and develop. They are shadows of themselves. They do not express themselves because they have no idea who they are, and they do not get what they want from life because they are short of skills and because they do not find out until it is too late what fulfills them. Young people who have no skills are ripe to be 'developed' by cults and persuasions which issue their messages forcefully enough. On a simpler level, people who have no voices of their own can hardly be heard in a world where the complexity of our communications system is so intricate that what is a crossed line to someone who is able, is a nightmare to someone who is not. That nightmare can, unfortunately, sometimes lead them to want to commit suicide.

Teenagers who want to, and in some cases do, commit suicide are a small but significant part of any columnist's postbag. Research tells us that both here and in the USA, the incidence of teenage suicide is rising. It is a pity that the incidence of adult understanding of this problem is not rising fast enough to cope with it. It is alarming that, as with the subject we label 'puppy love', teenage suicide is something which most adults cannot understand. They make comments like: 'She hadn't even given life a chance'; 'He was too young to know what he was doing'; 'What have they got to be despairing about at their age?' and 'They have all their lives ahead of them'.

It is precisely because they have all their lives ahead of them that some young people choose to die. If they can imagine life only as a continuance of present pain, then many bleak years of it stretching out into the future must be a ghastly and hopeless prospect. Saying that you cannot understand why they want to die is, once more, not to understand that young people are human, not to realize that they have emotions as we do. I cannot say that I would not want to die if I had a life of unemployment ahead of me living on the weekly pittance which is 'dole' money. To imagine that young people cannot know the hardships of life, that they do not really feel pain as we do, is to say that you cannot understand their despair. A friend who lives on a housing estate once said: 'I know why they do it. It's to stop themselves growing up like us lot.' And that could well be the answer to some suicides. Looking at the postures, expressions and habits of some of the adults around me I can see why a young person might take measures to avoid ending up like them.

Barbara was sixteen when she first wrote to me. She did not say she was suicidal but her letter implied it. It was a sad, depressed letter which explained, quite unemotionally in some ways, how she lived in a house alone with her father and thought she would not be able to take it much longer because they had not spoken to each other for eight months. Her father had thrown out her boyfriend because the latter had long hair and that is when the trouble started. Barbara vowed not to speak to her father again, and very soon after that he stopped speaking to her too.

As I said, the letter was undramatic in tone, but so dreadfully sad that I felt it needed immediate action. Barbara simply said that she had come to me as a last resort because she could not go on much longer. It was *my* feeling that she would not go on for much longer unless urgent help arrived. So I wrote by return of post asking her to call and see a friend of mine (a social worker at a teenage help agency) and phoned the friend at the same time saying that if she had not heard within four or five days to let me know. She did hear, within forty-eight hours, and saw the girl the same day. Within a week of that happening things were very different at Barbara's south London home. The social worker visited her school and, accompanied by Barbara's form teacher, then visited her home. Her form teacher had sensed something was wrong, but had not liked to pry and, since Barbara was a bright pupil who continued to work well, she had put her unease to the back of her mind. Through the visit to her home, Barbara was then reconciled with her father, which was such a relief to both of them that it was obvious Barbara would have no more problems about having longhaired friends thrown out of the house. I received two or three letters from Barbara after that. They tell their own story. Here is one of them:

Dear Carol,
Thanks for your letter you sent me at Christmas.
I hope you had a nice Christmas (although it's three months later) and a happy New Year.
Lot's has happened since the last letter, good as well as bad. Bad first: I've broken up with Steve, I knew it wouldn't work but I kept on hoping it would, it was over nothing, we just gradually stop seeing each other regular, and I decided I didn't want to go out with him any more so I phoned him and told him, and he ask to give it another try, but I said no.

Good now: I have decided to leave school this Summer, but I want to get a job as a Laboratory Technician, preferably as a Medical Lab Tech. I was wondering if you could help me in any way? I will be taking 7 'O' Levels in June in the following subjects: Mathematics, English Literature, English Language, Chemistry, Biology, Needlework and Antiquities. I will be taking a Spoken English Exam which will be graded but not counted as an 'O' Level. I am taking 1 C.S.E. in French and I have studied History and Geography for 4 years, Latin for 3 years, and Physics and Cookery for 2 years.

I have had some extra good luck. Have you ever heard of a Disco Club called CLOUDS CLUB I don't think you have, well it's in Brixton (it's not as bad as it sounds), I don't remember if I told you I went there every Sunday afternoon because there is an afternoon session for young people, any way I do. The Real Thing came down there. I have been crazy about them for the last 5 years. And then to see them in front of me, I tell you I would have fainted if it wouldn't have caused somebody some trouble.

They stood there and I couldn't stop staring. When I plucked up some courage I went up to them and said HELLO etc. To cut a long story short, I have just had the best days of my life so far. To be truthful I haven't recovered yet. I must be one of the luckiest people in the world because they have told me I can visit there office anytime I should wish, and if there up in London and they are not too busy I can see them. I've even got Ray Lakes phone no.

I must go now, sorry I took so long to answer your letter. Yours faithfully,

P.SP. Please write back soon. I am going to have my hair Permed. HEY you've never seen me have you? If you want to I send you a photo in the next letter one of me before and one of me after my perm. I hope it suits me.

Barbara is one of the few 'success' stories I can report from my attempts to help people to help themselves. For the most part I was aware that the young people who wrote to me needed far more assistance than I could offer. So I offered them what I had in the hope that some people would be helped, even if only a little, and there, for the most part, I had to leave it. But that was not the view of everyone. Since I live in an area of London where local talent still belongs to the community, it became a feature of everyday life to be approached by people who wanted help for their daughters, cousins, next-door neighbours, or any other young person who seemed as if they needed it. I would be approached in pubs, supermarkets, chemists, newspaper shops and even garages to ask if I could help with so-and-so's niece or if I knew anything that could be done for a girl who was taking drugs. It happened all to fit in well with a day's shopping or whatever else I was doing, and I enjoyed it. And since caring for people is a communal as well as a private activity and it is important that all people feel their help is worth giving and receiving, I would like to tell you the story of the way four of us once got together over three teenage boys who, on the face of it, needed no assistance at all.

The whole thing started with a phone call I had from a youth worker friend who asked if he could come round to chat about three of the boys in his youth club. One was sixteen and the other two were seventeen. He had begun wondering where they were getting their money from, because they were throwing an awful lot of it around. One day they took him into their confidence — they were all 'on the game'. My friend was nonplussed. When he rehearsed the arguments he could face them with, none of them stood up. He said: 'They've got me in a corner. What can I say? If I tell them they shouldn't be doing it they'll only laugh. They've got all the arguments on their side, and looking at it from their point of view, I can't blame them. They're earning over £200 a week tax-free, when they would be picking up dole money. They can lie in in the mornings. They don't have to get up and go to a nasty, smelly factory. They've got their freedom to do as they want. They don't have to say "yes" to a customer. Really, they're laughing. They're earning far more than I am if anyone's the mug they think it's me.'

The boys had apparently been prostitutes — for both men and women — for two or three months, and it was obvious that their parents were enjoying their money too much to worry about where it came from. Aside from the danger of catching VD, which the boys had been told about, I could see that they would imagine themselves to be in clover. And when you looked at the alternatives in their lives I could see why. All of them were virtually unemployable, even without an unemployment crisis, having left school with no qualifications or motivation to be anything. I could see no arguments that would be valid in their terms for deterring them. In fact, if I felt their choice were a free one, which it was not, and if they had been adults I might have seen no *reason* to deter them either; but that is another argument. For the moment both my friend and I were stuck. We both thought about it and said we would let each other know if we came up with anything. I, meanwhile, talked about the matter with various friends and contacts I thought might shed some light on it. One night I was talking with a man whose niece I had helped and he said: 'You should get Jerry [this is not his real name] to go and talk to them. He used to be a prostitute and he's got hair raising tales to tell about where it leads to.'

I rang up Jerry, who is a musician, and told him about the boys. He said he'd be happy to go down the club and see them, so we fixed it up. And it worked. Jerry is a local lad who thinks people like me 'talk posh, like' and when it comes to communicating with kids he knows what it's about. He said afterwards: 'I scared the shit out of them' and that was the end of the matter.

That sort of material could never have been used in the column which I wanted to expand so that I could get a few young helpers to assist me in running it. Unlike other agony columnists who deal with all age groups, I was fortunate in one way in receiving a postbag that was manageable — no more than about fifty letters a week. This meant that it was possible to reply to each letter personally and not send out the stereotyped replies that, because of the volume of their mail, other columnists have to send. I received a number of letters just thanking me for replying, and it seemed to me that the people who were writing had to have personal letters in reply. Therefore the plan I had decided to put forward if my mail became unmanageable was to have a teenage assistant to help me and therefore use the column as a way of providing one, or even a few, much-needed jobs for young people.

But I am afraid it never came to that because I became more and more disillusioned with running my column. It was being edited to such a degree that I felt it did not belong to me any more and it certainly did not belong to the people it was intended for — the teenagers who wrote in to it. It seems that an adult perception of what teenagers are, or should be, refuses to countenance them as they are. And letter after letter was being cut from the column because it did not fit into the mould of communication which the paper had decided was how communication should be. What was wanted, I was told, was letters that would interest people, that would give the column some zing.

I too felt the column lacked 'zing', but for the opposite reason to the editor. I felt it lacked 'zing' because it was beginning to lack authenticity and was being presented in typical media fashion, ignoring the fresh and individual way with which many of the young people I heard from expressed themselves. I became more and more dispirited about writing it and eventually we agreed to run it no more. The letters that came in after that I answered as a matter of course and gradually, except for John's, they stopped coming.

Some of the letters I received were sweet and others were very funny. They showed me that many important qualities get eroded by the process of growing up as we have organized it and I learned to ask why we have adults who are so inadequate that they lack the ability to love with anything other than disastrous consequences. Those consequences — disappointment, bitterness, jealousy, possessiveness — are then excuses not to love at all.

Reading between the lines of the letters I received there are many lovely, but unhappy young adults around. And while some of their letters would be undecipherable to anyone not used to reading the scraps of paper which come in, their overall message was clear: young people need a lot of help in finding themselves, and they are lost for the ability to ask for it.

7   The Sins of the Fathers

THE DESCRIPTIONS adults have given of how they themselves learned about sex go a long way towards explaining why the vast majority of young people whom I have met in classrooms have received no sex education at home. Adult friends, colleagues and parents with whom I have spoken in the last seven or eight years have told me stories of their own sexual conditioning which seem to belong to the last century not to this one. And while some of them vowed not to pass their sad experiences on to their children, many had not reconciled themselves with their sexuality until years after their children were born.

It has been particularly sobering to hear what men have said about their sexual conditioning. Without exception the men with whom I have spoken have said they were brought up to the implicit idea that sex is a 'doing' exercise. They have described their early sexual explorations as learning how to *do* something (mainly where to put their penis), unrelated to any idea of tenderness, sharing, consideration, or even happiness. One particularly distressing story was given by a father who is thirty-eight. He told of his sexual learning in the following way:

'When I was eight or nine I was playing with my girl cousins in the Anderson shed at the bottom of the garden: an "I'll show you mine if you show me yours" game. One of my aunts caught us at it, and there was a hell of a scene. I, as the only boy present, was subjected to a rigorous and hysterical interrogation about whether I had put it in. I had no idea then what sexual intercourse was, but it certainly *gave* me ideas. Even though I hadn't — and said so — I was thumped by my aunt and given a hiding by my father.

I first 'did it' when I was fourteen, with a girl older than me — she was fifteen — behind the graveyards near the school. I didn't know what to do. She took her knickers off and lifted up her skirt, so I took my trousers down and did as I was told, which was to lay on top of her. I thought it was a question of jabbing it in, but I couldn't do it. I realize now it was because I was so ignorant of female anatomy. I thought the hole was near where the lips meet. So she put it in for me. We did it a few times more over the weeks, but she got fed up with me. No doubt she found someone who could do it better. I really don't know what I felt about that incident. You ask me if it was pleasurable. I suppose it must have been, but I don't remember. I only remember the doing of it, and the feeling of accomplishment this gave me.

Aside from the beating at nine I "learned" nothing about sex or sexuality from my parents. And I'm afraid I knew nothing about female sexuality for many years. I got used to doing it standing up against walls, and I certainly never asked girls if they enjoyed it. There was no sharing, practically no conversation, and certainly no consideration. I knew nothing about appreciating women till I'd been having sex for many years. They were things you jabbed your willie into — if you were lucky. And you didn't respect the ones who let you do it to them because everyone said you married the ones who didn't.

Because of all this I was never comfortable with emotions. And I now see I had a terribly arrogant and condescending attitude towards women, which I'm still trying to shake off. There was no equality in any of my relationships with women: I was an emotional cripple. I still, all these years on, sometimes wince from the memory of the beatings, and I've made it my business to see that no child of mine grows up with the idea that their sexuality is bad. But not without a struggle, because most of the other adults my daughter comes across try to make her feel that her sexuality is bad and that she must be stopped from taking an interest in her body. I just wish I'd learned a lot earlier that women are not screwing machines, because I've learned most about the gentle things in life from women. I still have a lot of guilt about what I've done to women, and that, in itself, is arrogance. I just know that I screwed up rather a lot of people along the way to learning how to be a human being — including myself.'

So many men I have spoken with have said, categorically, that they have had to learn late in life how to respond to women as people and not to use them as objects. What is worrying is that our education of boys is still so backward — despite minor concessions to role-sharing like mixed cookery classes — that most of the boys I have met in classrooms have the same problem. They hide behind a shield of bravado — passed on to them by their fathers perhaps?

Another man now in his mid-forties, not himself a parent, gave the following account of learning about sex:

'The first thing I remember learning is that a man puts his willie in a girl's crack. I was about nine at the time, and one of the boys at school told me. Because I thought of my willie as being like a worm — another thing picked up from the boys in school — I thought sex was like putting a worm down a hole, and I didn't like the thought of that one bit. But that remained the extent of my sexual knowledge for some time. I need hardly say that I didn't learn anything from my parents. Who did?

My first sexual experience was frightening. It was in the back of a car parked on Dartford Heath, with the woman who afterwards became my wife. I was eighteen, and since I had never had sex before she showed me how. But I didn't manage it that night. I still kept on thinking about putting a worm in a hole. It's interesting when you look back on it. Sex was about doing, not feeling. As far as I was concerned it was a performance which I couldn't master. As our relationship went on, I managed it — the performance that is — but it wasn't something I wanted to do, it was something I felt I *should* do. Then I worked at doing it well, and we married by the time I was twenty-one.

I was twenty-nine before I first discovered how lovely sex really was. My marriage was falling apart, I was suffering terrible guilt and confusion and I met a woman who found me attractive. She let me know this and for the first time in my life I felt really excited sexually. I loved it, but it was frightening too. My marriage had been about the doing of it, whereas with this woman it was earthy, and I discovered what desire was. I also discovered what a clitoris was! Sex became a pleasure and I suddenly felt much lighter, as if a load had been lifted from me. And it affected me totally. I felt a new person. Previously I had been frightened of women because I feared sexual failure. I still do. I'm aware in my soul that I'm a very sexual person, yet I still think it's very important that I don't fail at it. This means I give confusing messages to people. I seem a sexual person and I seem friendly and confident in one way, but then I draw back.

Of course lack of information about sex mucks people up. I'm still tied to my past by it. And it's not only information that's missing, it's any idea of what good sex really is, that it's a beautiful way of sharing with another person. I never even thought about sex as sharing until I was in my mid-thirties. All this has affected me deeply, and I'm still picking my way out of it. I'm only thankful I didn't have children before I'd begun to sort it out, because there's no doubt they would have suffered, as I suffered at the hands of my parents, and they suffered at the hands of theirs. . . .'

The attitudes of the teenage boys I meet in schools still, all too unhappily, reflect tales such as these. The idea of sex as a mechanistic activity, not a sharing or feeling one, is brought out time and time again during the Word Game. The words given for sexual intercourse are usually doing words, not feeling words, so the minds of these young men are already shaped to the idea that sex is a doing activity, not a responsive one.

It is unfair, however, to suggest that all the descriptions adults have given of learning about sex have been horror stories, although I'm afraid most of them have been. One woman, who is in her sixties said she received no sex education whatsoever until she married — and that she and her husband have had a lovely time finding out together! Nevertheless, from observing her own children's lives, and those of her seven grandchildren, she comes down firmly in favour of sex education for young people. She said:

'I learned all I know from my husband. I've never slept with another man and we've had a fulfilled and happy marriage. It was during the menopause that this began to change. Frankly, I went right off sex — I gather a lot of women do during this time — and though we had had a good sex life I couldn't have cared less if we'd never made love again. Then my daughter bought me a book on the change of life, and it really opened my eyes. There were a lot of things in there we'd never even thought of, let alone done, and I learned about lubricating jellies and things like that too.

I got my husband to read the book — he wasn't too pleased about it, but he did, and things have been a lot better since then. What I hadn't realized was that he'd learned about sex from talking to other men, and that there was an awful lot he didn't know about. I'm sorry to say that it was he who spoke to our two boys about sex, and I now cringe to think what must have been said. It's certainly showed up in one of the boys' marriages. He has four children and, if I'm blunt, he didn't want any of them. He admits this himself now, but at the time he didn't know how not to have them. I feel very sad about it all, and while I know you can't change the past, I can see how it was all so unnecessary.

It is completely unnecessary for young people to be kept in the dark about the facts. As far as I'm concerned they should learn them as soon as they start asking questions. And it's not only the facts is it? Luckily my husband and I were never afraid to be affectionate in front of the children, so they've learned something from us, but really speaking I think I've learned more about life from my children than they've learned from me. I think it is marvellous that young people have much more open and equal relationships these days, and my own daughters have certainly taught me a great deal about how to improve my own relationship. Luckily I have a husband who has gone along with it. I don't envy young people these troubled times we live in, and as far as I'm concerned they need all the help they can get.'

It is obvious that facts given in isolation can be as meaningless as no facts at all. One woman, who is twenty-five, illustrated the dangers of this with a description of the euphemism which surrounded her discovery of a sanitary towel belt in her older sister's bedroom. She said:

was eight at the time, and I rushed downstairs to ask what this strange looking object was. I was immediately hurried off into the kitchen by my mum and my older sister and told 'the facts of life'. I can't remember most of what was said, it was like Double Dutch to me, but I do remember my mother saying that the egg inside a woman acted as a magnet for the man's sperm. And I thought I had an egg-sized magnet inside me! I was having trouble at the time with peeing when I got over-excited. So for quite a while I wore a large safety pin in my knickers because I thought the magnet inside me would draw it up into my vagina and stop the pee from coming out.

My parents never told me anything about sex and, naturally, or should I say unnaturally, they didn't display anything about sex. I mean I never saw them kissing, or holding hands or looking at each other in a special way. The only thing I do remember is that my mother began to get anxious about what I did with my friends. And I began to get the idea that there was something forbidden that was to do with men. And that's a pity, for after I left home I carried that with me. Without realizing it for a number of years I thought of men as sex objects. MAN meant possible danger and excitement; I didn't view men as people at all. I find it all very sad, the way people get so screwed up over sex, and it's all so completely unnecessary. It would be so simple for things to be different.'

Unfortunately, I don't think it would be simple, for the question of sex is not a simple, isolated one, but a complex human one. The inability of people to express themselves won't be changed overnight, for we are thwarted in this respect from quite a young age. Most of us are particularly thwarted in sexual matters, although one woman I spoke with escaped this. She said: 'We played doctors and nurses games from when I was quite young — about eight or nine. It was most enjoyable. I've never had any difficulties regarding sex, and I really feel that those early experiences were very good for me. Children naturally behave seductively and sensuously, I have seen it in my own children. We stopped playing sexual games when we entered puberty. I still feel my own experiences were very nice and innocent and I'm very glad I had them.'

A number of people spoke about these childhood experiences of touching and exploring, but for many, as with the man at the beginning of the chapter, those explorations ended up with a thrashing. With others, they were furtive affairs, ridden with guilt, and not at all the pleasant experiences they might have been. It is obviously difficult for adults to reconcile themselves to the incontrovertible fact that their children are sexual beings.

Only one of the people mentioned here was given a book to read to find out more about sex, although it is becoming more common for parents to give books to their children, or for young people to buy books themselves. This is probably because books on sexuality have become more accepted and, indeed, popular. It is unfortunate, therefore, that many of us working in sex education feel that a really first-rate book for teenagers has yet to be written. The FPA booklist on sex education contains just thirty titles, only a dozen of which are suitable for teenagers.

One of the latest of these is a book called *Talking Sex* by Miriam Stoppard, in which, by using the results of questionnaires given to teenagers, Ms Stoppard has tried to compile a book *for* teenagers rather than a book which talks *at* them. Personally I find the tone of the book ponderous and sometimes patronizing, and although it has some good things, like printing and discussing statements from teenagers themselves, there are a number of points which give cause for concern. Early on in the book she notes that the comments she has had from teenagers 'have shown conclusively that girls have a harder time of it during adolescence than boys.' To me those comments would indicate that the boys have been acting out their usual role — and furthermore, that Ms Stoppard has allowed them to get away with it. For my own observation tells me that it is boys who have a rather more difficult time, and that rather than admit this they hide behind comments which made them appear cool and okay — especially when filling in questionnaires!

Elsewhere, a rather unsubtle line drawing shows a naked female where an arrow proclaiming 'body hair' points only to the armpits and pubic areas. It would have been so simple to have allayed the fears of all girls who have hair round their nipples, a hairline from their navel down to their pubic hair, or heavy hair anywhere else on their bodies, to have stated that body hair is not uncommon in many areas. As it is, the idea that body hair on 'normal' women only exists in two places causes so much unnecessary suffering in girls. And why, oh why is this woman depicted in a cross between a demure and a traditionally glamorous pose, arm sweeping up her long hair, face turned modestly aside, eyes cast downward, while the man next to her gazes boldly at us?

It is a difficult task in so many ways to write a book on sexuality for teenagers, and it is not surprising that few succeed. In the

FPA we have to be so careful about what we say to a young person, lest it be taken out of context and used against us, that it would be a brave person indeed who would actually WRITE IT DOWN. Yet teenagers' reading is, from what pupils tell me, little monitored by parents. Girls come into school with the most awful pulp, in the form of popular teenage magazines. We sometimes examine the contents, and they're crammed full of romantic fiction of the 'panting breaths' and 'her resisting till she can hold out no longer' variety. And while I'd like to think that most of the soft porn which the boys read is bought without their parents' permission, I'm concerned that, for a few at least, this reading is part of an 'all boys together' pact with their fathers. 'I won't tell your mum on you if you don't tell on me.'

One brave person who *has* tackled the subject of teenage sexuality frankly and without constraint is Jane Cousins whose book, *Make It Happy* was written specifically for teenagers as a result of conversations and interviews with hundreds of young people. When the book came out in 1978, the FPA welcomed it as the most comprehensive work of its kind and we took it into schools with us — until we were banned from doing so. Two sections of the book — on bestiality and incest — were deemed, by certain Junior Ministers, to be scandalous and, reluctantly, we had to stop using the book.

I have however seen it still being used in some schools and the staff with whom I have spoken have said it is eminently sane and sensible. My own opinion is that this is the best work available for teenagers. It goes much further than any other British book, both pictorially and in general content, to present an overview of sexuality in a clear, interesting and unpatronizing way. For that reason, many pupils have wanted to read it. They may be attracted by the fact that the book is well laid out with some *real* photographs of teenage bodies, not just drawings of them, and that it has a vitality and reality about it which is appealing. I personally do not object to the five or six lines in which bestiality is described, for a significant number of young people ask what this word means and straight information must be preferable to imagination. The tone of most of this book is admirably neutral, but it does concern me that approval is implied for a passage on masturbation where it is stated that young people like to masturbate with a finger up their anus. I feel it would have been better to have put no value judgement on this, or to have been discouraging, since this form of masturbation creates a risk from infection from the bacteria in the rectum. However, *Make it Happy* is still the most comprehensive and fair book I have come across, and one from which teenagers I have spoken with have benefited by reading.

The FPA has its own booklet, *Learning to Live with Sex*. It is clear and succinct, but there is, for example, no picture of the female genitalia, although the clitoris is described under the general heading 'Climax'. I feel that the drawings in *Learning to Live with Sex* are also rather old-fashioned. It serves a useful purpose in the classroom. I'm just not sure that many young people would read it outside school.

Amongst the other books for teenagers are a couple of paperbacks called *Boys and Sex* and *Girls and Sex*, both by Wardell B Pomeroy. The books are sound as far as they go, and their tone is pleasing, but they contain no pictures or diagrams, and I feel that this is a distinct handicap in presenting material to young people.

What is needed in a book for teenagers is a combination of accurate, comprehensive and sensitively-gathered information with a tone which is pleasant and nondidactic. Yet the book which has come nearest to providing this — *Make It Happy* — is the one which has been most criticized. It has been criticized, in particular, by people who feel that sex education is a family affair. It is obvious that no book is as satisfactory as the experience of growing up in a home where affection, responsibility and concern for others are visibly present. However, where the example of a mature, loving relationship between adults is not available as a learning experience for children, other sources need to be found. Ideally, of course, books would be a supplement to what children already learned from home, and if children *were* learning from parents, adults would have less to fear from what children learned elsewhere. What is clear is that far too many children derive the bulk of their learning from 'elsewhere'.

The way adults have themselves learned about sexuality goes a long way towards explaining why this is the case. There is a chain reaction from generation to generation passing on the unsavoury bonds of ignorance, and fear.

8 People in Launderettes Don't Catch VD

THE CONTENT of my sex education lessons is as varied as the number of lessons I have taken: no two have been identical. Topics have covered lead in petrol; the babies' dried milk scandal; the politics of fashion, and 'Are we really overcrowded or is that a nasty rumour?' We have discussed male aggression in sexuality; whether sex is a spiritual experience; whether wearing certain clothes makes women more likely to be attacked; what to do if a boy gets a girl pregnant and she wants to keep the baby and he does not. We have talked about being in love and loving, and the differences between the ways we love different people. We have found that with human behaviour it is difficult to make binding rules and that it is often difficult to work out what we really feel.

It is people's feelings I am concerned about when entering a classroom. And since this is the case, it means that as no two lessons have been identical in content, neither have they been identical in approach. People often ask about 'approach' and, again, the answer is not easy to give in just a sentence or two. There is no doubt that it is the quality of relationship between myself and pupils which is an intrinsic part of the answer — but how does that come about? My side of it involves entering a classroom *prepared*, in fact desiring, to learn from pupils. This means striving to be exceptionally aware and listening without appearing to do so for all the signs that twenty strangers give you of how they feel about themselves, about each other and about you. The best description I heard of this awareness was given in a television programme by Dorothy Heathcote, who is well known for her drama work with children and adults. She described a good teacher as being like a cat, extraordinarily light of foot and able to change direction with ease and grace. Two comments of hers I particularly value are: 'You must trust the children to teach you what to say', and, 'When the work is bigger than you or the class, then you're sailing.'

There have been times when the work has been bigger than all of us, when the quality of relationship has carried us along in its own tide. For my part this has been made possible by my own acute awareness of what is happening around me, my respect for the group and the work, and the way in which young people chasten and enliven me so that I am rarely caught flat-footed.

For their part, young people have an extraordinary way, despite their often difficult lives, of giving of themselves and of providing the energy and humour for us to work with. From the 14-year-old boy who responded to the question: 'Do you think you have been indoctrinated with sexual values?' with the wry answer: 'Yes, Miss, I have received an indoctrination of silence', to the 15-year-old who in answer to his friend's question defined an orgy as 'an over-exuberant party', their comments have educated me to a keen appreciation of their world — and of my own. It is that appreciation which makes it possible for me, a stranger, to join their groups and to have discussions which are affectionate and educative rather than fearful and embarrassing.

One particular lesson which stands out in my mind developed after we had been discussing holding and cuddling. I had been trying to work out why people are cuddled less when they are older and why boys in particular are deprived. We had discussed the many different circumstances in which holding a person is a non-sexual act and were wondering why most people do not hold each other and how their lives might alter if they did. One boy asked what all this had to do with sex education (he was obviously interested in getting down to brass tacks) so I asked him if he could see no connection at all. He said he could not, so I asked him what aspects of sex education he was interested in learning about and he replied: 'Fucking, Miss.'

There was a buzz of voices round the group at his bluntness, but there were no objections when I asked if anyone minded if we discussed 'fucking'.

I next asked the boy why he wanted to know about fucking and he said: 'Cos that's what it's about, Miss.'

I asked him how he knew that and he said because his older brother had told him, so I asked if he would mind telling us about the sex education he had received from his older brother. He did not, and his story went like this:

> 'Well, I caught my brother and his girl doing it, you know, fucking, 'cept I didn't know what it was. I was eleven, see, and he was much older than me. I asked him

afterwards what he was doing and he said it was "fucking" and I said: "What's that?" and he told me.'

'Told you what?'

'What fucking is, Miss.'

'Yes, but what exactly did he say?'

'He said it's when a man puts his cock in a woman's hole, and I said to him: "What hole, man?" and he said: "The one in the middle and you have to make sure you put it in the right one because a woman's got three holes." '

'Did he tell you anything else?'

'Yes, he said when I felt something, as if I was going to pee, I must take my cock out.'

'Did he tell you why?'

'No, Miss.'

'Did you ask him?'

'No.'

'Did you ever learn anything else about sex from your family or your friends, or from school?'

'Yeh, I learned you musn't get the girl pregnant.'

'How do you stop that happening?'

'By pulling your cock out, Miss.'

If every class contained a person who would describe to you so realistically such rudimentary sex education it would be a great help. It would not stir anyone very much if I stated: 'Sex without feelings can be very disappointing', but this boy's flat description of the act certainly affected the rest of the group. 'That's not what sex is about,' they protested.

'Well, what is it about?' I asked. 'Come on, let's build up a picture of what sex is about.'

There were a few tentative offers, but no one was very forthcoming, so I asked why and one of the girls said: 'It's because we don't know enough, Miss.'

So we had a discussion of what you had to 'know about' in order to understand sex, and we came up with 'feelings' and 'touching' and I asked the group if they felt they had any experience in either of these two areas. They said they had, but it was 'different', so I asked them all to close their eyes.

We were sitting in complete circle. I started to speak very quietly, asking them to keep their eyes gently closed, and said I was going to walk round slowly and touch each one of them. In other circumstances I have had a mock stampede start at this point, but the group was happy to go along with it. I walked round and, speaking softly all the time, touched each person, on their shoulder, on their hand, on their arm or on their head. I asked them to relax and to just enjoy, or if they did not enjoy it, just think quietly about what was happening and what they were feeling about it. At the end, before they all opened their eyes I said something like: 'The reason for doing this is to show you that we are all born with feelings of tenderness and quiet pleasure which we seem to ignore as we get older. We are able to enjoy being gently touched, but would usually not admit this, even if it happened to us, I wonder why?'

It was obvious that people opened their eyes reluctantly.

'Have you learned anything about feelings?' I asked.

'Yes,' said one girl. 'I didn't know how nice it was to have my arm touched. I can't ever remember that happening before.'

From there the discussion took the shape of people talking about how they felt and why they did not usually feel that way. I asked them if they felt touching had anything to do with sex, and they began to realize what I was implicitly saying: that they had the authority and the ability to discuss relationships and did not need my permission to do so.

We then looked at some of the problems that arose from our earlier definition of sexual intercourse as something which happens when 'a man puts his cock in a woman's hole'. Could we now begin to discuss what was missing from this description? We could, and we did some rôle-play of people approaching each other to try and get to know each other. And I then dealt with the business of the 'three holes', which is as much a relief to the boys in the class as it is to the girls. This is one of the rare occurrences in life when they are not pleased to be spoiled for choice!

There was a sigh when the double period eventually ended. 'We're getting places,' I said. 'See you next week.' Which is when one boy said: 'We may all be in *The News of the World* before then.'

'Whatever for?' I asked.

'Well,' he said. 'If Mary Whitehouse could have seen you then, Miss, there's no way you'd have explained your way out of it. . . .'

Most of the work in sex education is involved with just this kind of material — the experiences, fears and feelings which make up people's lives — and it is this that we have to work with. My role is to create an environment where this can happen safely. It was obvious that this group was, in the main, strongly opposed to the idea that sex is a crude, mechanical process, and they needed some other way of defining it. I therefore felt — from them — that it was all right to 'risk' some tenderness. Had that 'risk' not been right for the group we would still have been in a safe place. We would probably have discussed why it is difficult to be touched, and may have realized why sex *is* so often couched in crude terms.

It is an indictment of our values that I should use the word 'risk' together with the word 'tenderness'. There is a problem with touching people in a classroom to which I am very sensitive, and there is also a problem with associating sex with tenderness. Could this session have been used as an example of how sex educators lead young people astray by encouraging them with ideas that sex is a warm, pleasant, tender experience which they might like? The reason why I took the 'risk' was that the form teacher was present in this group, and where a staff member is present I am generally more confident, for there is a witness to what has happened: there is a person to balance the one bright spark who goes home and says: 'The sex educator lady touched us up today!'

If some of the teenagers I teach have basic or sketchy knowledge about our subject, others have some extraordinary ideas about sex. I recall in particular one boy, in a mixed class at a large comprehensive. I was about to give some information about VD when he stopped me and said: 'I know how you get VD, Miss.'

> 'How's that?' I asked.
> 'From caterpillars, Miss.'
> I was about to laugh, but realized he was not joking, and I asked him to tell me about it.
> His story went like this: 'VD is carried by "special" flying caterpillars which come from strange lands and land on your clothes while they are hanging on the line. When you put on your clothes you then get VD.'
> I asked the boy where he had heard about this and he said he read it in the paper last week.
> I thought I would get him to see the error of his ways and said: 'This sounds very odd to me. Let's look at it. For a start, I have never heard of caterpillars which fly.'
> 'They're special ones, Miss, they come from Africa.'
> 'But how can they fly all the way from Africa? It's thousands of miles.'

'I told you they're special, Miss,' he said stubbornly.

Thinking I had the answer at last I asked, with an edge of triumph, 'If they land on your clothes on the line, what about people who use launderettes?'

His reply flattened me: 'People in launderettes don't catch VD, Miss.'

I wish that were the strangest notion I have come across, but it is not. People who imagine you insert The Pill in your vagina, girls, and boys, who imagine you have intercourse through the navel, people who believe sperm will drop out if you jump up and down still exist. And that is without thinking about really complex sexual issues like feelings, morality etc. Sometimes in order to get a particularly recalcitrant group to think about these issues you have to work very hard. I am thinking, in particular, of a group of a dozen nearly sixteen-year-old boys who were literally waiting to leave school. I was a 'soft option' and they were not in the least bit interested in doing anything — or at least that is what they were trying to convey to me.

Their response to anything I asked was either a yawn or 'Why are we bothering with all this?' I fished around in my own mind for something which would intrigue or interest them. So I asked them what they would feel like if they saw a partner who really attracted them, say a girl at a party, and the night after they saw her she came round to their home and said she was willing to have intercourse. After the predictably crude replies, a few of the boys were, as I had hoped, moved sufficiently to say that this would be too easy and that they wouldn't like it. They actually said that it would be no fun unless they had to 'work' to get her. We then got on to discussing the subject of work. Why would they not appreciate a girl unless they worked for her? What was the difference between that kind of 'work' and other kinds of work? How important was work? We eventually ended up trying to find out what life was for if it wasn't for work.

In a session like this I am doing all the running, which is not the way I like it, but is preferable to doing nothing at all. In an attempt to gain interest, I use a great deal of stimulus in terms of changing my position often, changing the tone and pitch of my voice a great deal, and often switching from active to still, loud to quiet, quite abruptly. I do this because with your ear firmly to the ground, in this group all you can hear is the sound of torpor from the trenches these boys have dug themselves into so that life doesn't catch them with a direct hit. So I use a great deal of physical movement in an attempt to cause some seismic upheavals. I realize that if a video were taken of the class it would look as if I were putting on a show, and this is what it feels like to me. But my ultimate objective is engagement, initially in the form of 'audience' participation and eventually in the form of leaving the stage and letting them speak for themselves. This worked to a small degree in this group, because although the going was all uphill, it did end up in me sitting down and in them feeling prompted enough to begin discussing the meaning of life!

I know that in three double lessons those boys and I did no sex education as anyone would recognize it. There was no point. They were too impoverished to care sufficiently about themselves to ask for help. And the attitude they give is misleading because it does not depict what they are feeling, only what they have tried to use as protective cover. I would like to illustrate this point with the story of a boy whom I shall call Tony.

Tony was in a truancy centre because by the age of fourteen, when I met him, he needed one-to-one attention. At first glance he was one of the most unattractive people I have ever met. Such was his armour of aggression that Tony, seen as he was during my first visit, would have deterred the most assiduous helper. He did not know who his father was and his mother did not want him and refused to take care of him. He seemed to have two extreme options: either he could cry at the awfulness of his life or he could fight furiously and bitterly. He chose the latter. He screamed, hurled himself around the room, shouted and flung himself about, all to a stream of invective.

'She's fucking posh, isn't she. What's all this then?' he said, aggressively flicking up the loose sleeve of my jumper in a contemptuous way. (It was interesting he spoke about, and not to me).

'This then,' I said, 'is the sleeve of a jumper that has more wool in it than most sleeves.'

'What's it bleeding for then?' he demanded.

'To make work for sheep,' I replied.

'She's stupid an' all,' he mocked.

And so it carried on, with Tony prancing up and down the room, until he eventually got too much for Ted, the organizer, who insisted that Tony went upstairs with him to have a few things out. They left together. I gathered from the other workers that the centre was having enormous difficulty trying to contain Tony but, as one of them said: "If *we* fail then he is out on his own. There'll be nowhere left for him to go after us.'

What had really infuriated them was that Tony's mother had just had yet another unwanted baby at the age of thirty-four. One of them said: 'You try taking Tony back to her doorstep and telling her he's her responsibility and she laughs in your face; and here she is, 'proud mum' all over again.'

Before leaving, I wanted to see Ted and, thinking he and Tony had finished, went upstairs. Ted and Tony were facing each other with the drawn and pale looks of people who have been involved in a bitter conflict: they were both emotionally spent. Tony's parting shot as I walked in was: 'Fuck the world, mister, and you too.' Ted walked by me, with a look of defeat on his face, and I went to follow him.

The whispered word was barely audible, but it had been said: 'Miss. . . .'

I turned round and Tony was standing, his fists clenched, facing the window, his body heaving with sobs that had overtaken it. As I walked towards him, he turned to me and I remember thinking that he looked about as ugly as I have ever seen anyone look in all my life: his face was twisted in anguish. And I loved him. As I reached him, he hurled himself at me, burrowing his face into my midriff and I found I was sobbing with him. We stayed like that for a while, both crying until he said, drawing himself away: 'Don't tell anyone, will you?'

That gave me a serious problem: What do you do about information given in confidence, the divulging of which breaks trust and the withholding of which keeps from helpers information which may be vital? On other occasions, as I saw Tony launch himself at the people who were on his side, it was like watching someone destroy himself, and doing nothing to help. He exacted revenge upon himself with a ferocity that was determined and heartbreaking. So I told Ted, and he was pleased that I did. It gave him the strength to carry on loving someone whose way of putting himself beyond help (of destroying himself) was to try to make himself unlovable.

At a conference I once attended called 'Accepting Adolescent Sexuality', James Hemming described part of an adult's responsibility to young people with the following words: 'When you are young, life is full of moving walls. It is important for people who have no boundaries to be given them. We have a duty to stop the walls moving, to let young people know where they stand in relation to their surroundings.'

An authoritarian would leap on that statement with cries of 'I told you so. We have to put them in their place', but I do not think letting people know where they stand is an exercise in repression. Rather it is an exercise in devotion. If we were really devoted to our children we would help them with their walls, we would be there like sceneshifters, ready to bring on another prop if it would assist the process of enquiry. Tony's walls were not there and he was so accustomed to desolation that when someone tried to build them for him he sabotaged the attempt. We are so shortsighted that we blame him for his acts of violence rather than look to ourselves for the reason why a child is so emotionally orphaned.

In another classroom a group of sixteen-year-olds are slumped over their desks.

'Why don't you like yourself, Millie?'

'I do, Miss.'

'Then why are you abusing your body?'

'I'm not, Miss,' she protests hotly.

'Well, look at what you're doing to it at the moment. Your shoulders, Millie, they look as if they were born in the last century, and your stomach looks fedup and your face! It looks as if you're determined not to enjoy yourself at all costs. . . . 'Hasn't anyone ever heard of panache?' I ask.

'Please, Miss, what's panache?'

'It's what you lot haven't got right now. And it's free. Doesn't cost a penny, doesn't hurt, and it's there for the asking. . . . 'That,' I say, gliding towards the blackboard, 'is panache and this [making myself look as sensual as a stick of limp celery], isn't. Now what does the dictionary say?

'Your body talks, you know,' I tell a sceptical looking audience. 'It speaks volumes. It's telling me you're beginning to wake up. Don't try and hide yourselves. Come on. They're your bodies, nobody else's. We see that it is not only by words that we communicate, but by many means.'

What is really disturbing is young people's and, indeed, most adults' unawareness of this. As human beings we are well equipped to communicate, and yet we do so little real communicating or engaging. Most of it is a superficial, parrying activity. So many of the young people I have met suffer from what seems to be premature *rigor mortis* of the emotions. They are so locked up, and they need an unlocking process which will not endanger them. At the end of this particular session we played a game where we tried to guess people's feelings from their body posture and their expressions, and from this game the group began to wake up. We then played a kind of charades, but with feelings, where one person came into the room and mimed a feeling for the rest of us to discover.

The whole session was an attempt to introduce young people to the idea of communication; through their bodies, their faces, their gestures and their words. And from that to introduce them to the idea that learning to express themselves is vital in their lives. The following week, I remember, we tried to work out what were the factors in their lives that made it less easy for them to express themselves and they came up with: parents (most), teachers (some), television programmes, having no brothers and sisters, and being shy.

Yet we always come back to words, and I know how surprised parents would be if they heard some of the traditional inform-ation which their children freely give. In a discussion on re-sponsibility, for example, the problem of old people is so often brought up.

'Who are we responsible for?' I ask a group of fifteen-year-olds.

'For sick people, and for people who can't help them-selves and for old people. They shouldn't have to go into homes, you know?'

'Who should look after them, then?'

'The family. It's the family's responsibility. They should do something about it.'

'But can you force people to do things?' What if the family don't care?'

'They should be made to care.'

'Would you like to be made to do something? How many of you like being forced into things?'

SILENCE.

'So what are we going to do about old people if we can't force people to care for them?'

Then there was the only time I have ever sent anyone out of a class. It was a mixed group, and the 'antics' of one boy strongly resembled those of an energetic monkey. He was incredibly dexterous at managing to make about a hundred disruptive movements a minute without actually getting out of his seat. And this was coupled with the ability to make non-stop sounds of seemingly infinite variety. Certainly a major distraction and one I couldn't cope with. So I asked him to report to his form master.

At the end of the lesson, the master, who is an energetic and sympathetic teacher said: 'Graham's outside. He wants to have words with you.'

I asked if he had sent the boy to see me, and he said: 'No, I just told him he was pretty stupid to get himself sent out of a sex education lesson when you come to the school to try to help him.'

So I went out into the darkened corridor where Graham was standing and said: 'I'm sorry I had to exclude you from the class. It makes me seem a failure as a teacher. . . .'

Before I could go any further the boy, who was fourteen, burst into tears. He kept on saying how sorry he was and how he did not want to upset me, and I ended up comforting him by telling him that I was really quite all right!

When I spoke with the form master afterwards he told me that Graham had a very unpleasant home life, with a father who was heavy-handed with him and everyone else in the family, including the mother. The reason for his behaviour was that he could not cope with the emotions that were being discussed. He could not cope with gentleness without becoming emotional himself, without, in other words, crying for himself and his hard life. So he was disruptive instead. It seems sometimes that there is no end to the pain you find in classrooms.

At another school, a comprehensive about ten miles outside London, there is another boy I shall never forget — but for quite a different reason. He, again, was a live wire, but with a scarcely veiled warmth and earnestness to learn. After every session he asked me if he could help carry my bags to the car and, as we walked, I waited for him to ask whatever it was he needed to know. And eventually he did ask: surprisingly, in front of the whole group. He asked the question which most of the pupils I have met would like to ask, and either can't or daren't.

'How is making love nice, Miss?'

No one laughed. No one moved. They all waited for the answer. I thanked him for giving me the opportunity to try to reply to that particular question, but said that I couldn't do it alone. I asked the group to move closer, and we brought our chairs round, the form mistress included, into a much tighter circle. And there we sat, for the rest of the afternoon, huddled in this way leaning forward in earnest discussion. We talked about love, fear, pleasure, pain, anxiety and joy — particularly joy.

In this group we discussed the joy of sharing, but young people's main experience of early sex is through masturbation, which is a subject that we spend quite a bit of time discussing in some groups. One of the best comments I heard on the subject was from a person who said: 'You have to admit it, Miss, most of the "comes" in the world are had that way.' The subject of masturbation is a difficult one to deal with because as a common sexual practice it is the most shunned. Adults will now talk with each other about sexual intercourse, and make jokes about 'getting laid last night', but we are still not comfortable talking about masturbation. Yet masturbation is as much a part of adult sex as it is of young sex, even if not indulged in so frequently. Because of the way most women have orgasms, masturbation is a common part of a couple's love play, and mutual masturbation is not uncommon during the advanced stages of pregnancy, during menstruation, or simply at times when you feel like it. Despite this, the subject is still an embarrassing one. People who are able to tell their children the 'facts of life' are not able to tell them the facts of masturbation.

Talking about masturbation in the classroom has these, and one other problem. Usually, when discussing sexual activity I talk about it as something which the teenagers in the group have not yet arrived at. With masturbation I am aware that it cannot be discussed this way: it is something which is already happening, yet I do not want anyone to be threatened by the fact that I know this. So the way I usually begin is: 'Masturbation is ordinary. . . .'

From there it is not then difficult to find ways of discussing how masturbation plays a part in adult sex, how it is not therefore just something that young people do before they have 'proper sex' and how it does not spoil your chances of having 'proper sex' unless you take it to extremes. What is really interesting is that there has never been a class which has told me that female masturbation is ordinary too. A few people have said they think girls masturbate, but by far the majority of teenagers imagine that masturbation is a male preserve. The biology textbooks make their point. There may, if you are fortunate, be a picture of the urethral opening, and the vaginal passage, but the clitoris is nowhere in evidence. In a map of the female anatomy, the clitoris might as well be a place in Outer Mongolia. This arrangement is, of course, a sound way of keeping girls from discovering the pleasures of sex, but can it be right to keep from them the whereabouts of a part of their body? They may learn about the anus, the pancreas and the lymph gland, but let them not know that they possess something called a clitoris.

It is therefore not surprising that the vast majority of girls I have spoken with have no idea they possess this 'thing'. They do not know that a woman may masturbate if she chooses. The boys usually know slightly more about female anatomy than the girls do, but too many of them view the clitoris as something, like a meccano set, that they have to get to work.

'The human body is not a bit of machinery,' I explain. 'You don't just press bits here and get automatic responses.'

This is often the boy's mechanistic approach to sex, and it is most worthwhile in a mixed group to enable everyone present to see this. The boys tend to think of it as a doing activity whereas the girls still think of it as a being done unto, or a feeling activity.

'How do you suggest we bridge this gap?' (silly question when you think about it) I asked one group of sixthformers.

'With a space rocket,' came a wry reply. As another sixthform girl said: 'Doesn't it strike you as odd, Miss, that we've travelled to the moon, been through the sound barrier and invented robots, while half the people in this class didn't know what a clitoris was?'

'I find it decidedly odd,' I said.

'There is a conspiracy to prevent us discovering ourselves,' said a flamboyant gentleman in the back row.

'Those are wiser words than you'll ever know,' I answered. 'Why do you think it exists?'

'To stop us all running riot,' says another person.

'But why would us knowing ourselves be riotous,' I ask. 'What are the implications of the alternative to that?'

One girls asks, interestingly, when the clitoris was discovered, and people laugh.

'I honestly don't know,' I answer. 'But it's a fair question, isn't it? How have we got to hear about it?'

This leads into a discussion of the part the women's movement and science (with the offering of relatively safe contraception) have played in awakening us to the fullness of female sexuality.

'What does that say about absolutes?' I ask.

'That they're variable,' comes a reply. 'Things are only absolute according to the age you're living in.'

'You're absolutely right — or are you?' I ask. 'What may we discover from this perplexing state of affairs?'

The subject is still sex education, or at least it was. Is it still? I think so. Philosophy has as much place in sexuality as anywhere else and if we are sexual beings can we separate our lives from our sexuality?

'I thought you were here to give us some answers,' said one boy, smiling. 'To give us some information about contraception and abortion and all that.'

'How can I give you answers about your own sexuality?' I replied. 'Certainly I will give you some standard information, but whose life is it that you have there? Can I answer it for you?'

There it is in a nutshell. The subject of sex education is as varied as the thoughts, feelings and affections of the people I meet and the person I am. I find myself at adult gatherings seemingly moronically incapable of describing to anyone what I teach, for I have no rules or syllabus to teach by. There is a code, of course, of which I am aware, which says, simply, that I do not want to damage anyone or to have anyone damaged as a result of meeting me, or as a result of an exchange in any of the groups I have been in. The main tool at my disposal in trying to avoid this is my affection for others, and for myself.

9 The Ostrich Position

ONE OF the most daunting things which happened to me in a school was when a deputy headmaster came up just before the pupils came into the classroom and said: 'I would like you to know from the start that I am dead against sex education. The rest of the staff are well aware of my objections. I intend to sit in on this lesson to see what happens.'

Teaching is not an easy task in most circumstances. Under the conditions of that morning I felt it was intolerable. I was aware that every word, every gesture, was being watched, for a hint of . . . what exactly? And the only way I could see round the problem was to 'fail' honourably. So I behaved in the same way I would usually. I did not shy away from touching a pupil in case the action was misunderstood, or from playing the Word Game. The pupils were subdued — obviously as a result of having the deputy head present — but became absorbed enough for us all to forget his presence as the relationship between us developed. I was therefore astonished when at the end of the lesson the deputy head came up, shook me warmly by the hand and thanked me. He was, he said, quite moved by what he had seen and had no further reservations about my teaching the subject. I asked him why he had no reservations when he had heard four-letter words uttered. He answered: 'It wasn't the words I was worried about, but the feelings. So much of this stuff is taught clinically.'

So the man was not, as I had imagined, a bigot, but someone who was concerned, as I imagine we all are, that a discussion of feelings is absent from many sex education courses.

Close surveillance was the keyword in an even more disturbing situation at another large London comprehensive. We had been invited in by the biology mistress who could not cope with the questions she was being asked by her pupils. She had approached the headmistress to ask for sex education to be provided, and the head had refused. There was to be no sex education going on in her school. Two girls in the biology mistress's class were, from what she could gather, sleeping with their boyfriends. The head was approached again and her reply was: 'It's not our fault if this is going on. It's the parents'.'

Whether or not that is true it is, I hope you will agree, a short-sighted and inhumane way for anybody concerned with education to behave. However, under further pressure, this particular headmistress agreed she would allow the teaching of personal hygiene in her school — but not sex education. The biology mistress then decided to act. She called us up and asked us to come and speak — disguised as health visitors. While the real purpose of our visit was sex education, the topic on my form said: 'Personal Hygiene'.

I was not at all happy about this. It is bad enough to know how much criticism you attract as a sex educator. It is even worse to stoop to pretending you are not one. But the biology mistress won me round. She was very concerned about her pupils and was doing the best that she could for them under difficult circumstances. She implored me if I met the head in the corridor not to tell her what I was doing. When I expressed anxiety about the possibility of her coming into one of my classes I was told not to worry 'she never does that'.

During the break I had a chat with another teacher who said: 'What goes on in this school, and in fact in the GCE syllabus, is utterly ridiculous. We teach them the heart, the liver and the respiratory system of a human being and the reproductive organs of a bloody rabbit. No wonder they get some odd ideas about sex.'

The 'oddness' is, I am afraid, reinforced in many schools, once you venture behind the gates. It is alarming that some heads view us as the people you bring in when all else has failed, and the sight of a gaggle of girls admiring a schoolfriend's baby greeted me at one school I visited. This was in one of my favourite schools where the pupils are lively and the staff are interesting and caring — except that is, for the headmaster. He has, to this day, refused to meet me, despite the fact that I visited his school for five years running and once also did regular counselling sessions under the pastoral care programme. He has let his deputy know that he does not care to meet me because he thinks it would be 'inappropriate'. His position, in my opinion, is doubly ostrich-like. When danger threatened (in the form of some of his pupils getting pregnant) he buried his head in the sand, and when other members of his staff decided to act (by calling us in) he decided not to recognize us. So he 'turned a blind eye' as we entered the school gates and presumably absolved himself from the responsibility of our being in his school.

He presumably has strange ideas about what sex education is and about what it is for. He perhaps imagines it is some kind of emergency service which you call in, like the fire brigade, when things are getting out of control. I imagine his conception of my work is that I 'do' some sort of contingency reading of the riot act: I let the sexually active know about contraception, abortion and VD, and use the latter to warn the people who are not doing it of the penalties. I am not too explicit about what 'it' is in case I encourage the 'not yet thinking about doing it' section into premature activity. This farcical picture of our function makes me feel like a fumigator called in to deal with a health hazard. It is not easy to live with the fact that, professionally, you are less welcome than a pest control officer.

The fact that I have only met the heads or deputy heads of four out of fourteen schools I have been in worries me. And in eight years of teaching, only one school has invited me to meet the staff to discuss what we do. In that particular school the headmaster asked me to address a meeting of the staff about the nature and purpose of our work, and they afterwards asked questions or expressed their reservations. I do not think it is a coincidence that pupils in that school are a credit to their teachers. The school is also an example of what can be done through discernment and sound organization.

It had had a very poor reputation before the present head took over and its pupils reflected this. The school itself is a shambles of old, depressing buildings and pupils were apt to run wild. When I first visited, a colleague had to break up a very unpleasant fight that was taking place in the school corridors, and there was a general air of apathy and ignorance. To go into that school is now a pleasure. Although the buildings are the same, the place is the cleanest school I visit, and the pupils are a joy to be with: they are boisterous and friendly and you are greeted as you walk along the corridors with smiles, and cries of 'Hello, are you coming back to us this year?'

The remarkable change in this school proves to me that if you are a good enough educator, a good enough organizer and a person of vision, pupils will learn. It also proves that if you are not these things they will not learn. In other words, what a school is like depends upon its staff, and there are a number of teachers whose skill and dedication you can only marvel at. I am thinking in particular of one woman who began, single-handed in a boys' school, a programme of sex education which has been running for six or seven years. She is such a remarkable person that the boys feel able to talk with her about their fears and problems without worrying about facing her as a teacher in the next lesson and without worrying that she will in some way penalize them.

But there is no doubt that the provision of sex education is generally in chaos. Only a few schools have what I would call full programmes of sex education undertaken by the staff, and others pay no more than a token gesture to the subject. One school in south London considers the subject to be so important that the whole staff is involved in making sure that adolescent sexuality is accommodated, helpfully. Anne Jones, the head who instigated the programme at Vauxhall Manor Secondary School described how:

'In the first year we have a three-week course in simple sex education: the plain facts, contraception included. As with any other set of facts, our pupils begin to grasp their wider relevance as they get older. Then throughout the whole of the fourth year (fourteen- to fifteen-year-olds) we run a health education course which covers all manner of things — diet, first aid, child development, smoking, drugs — and sex education is included here because it's all geared towards physical and emotional well-being and social health. We talk about things generally rather than using a text book approach. We'll use a TV programme or a film as stimulus and then break into group discussion afterwards. We also welcome informal questions from the pupils or their requests to have chats about 'things generally'. The pupils seem to seek out whichever teacher they feel they, personally, can talk to. It's quite complicated from the staff's point of view, but we're all agreed it's important to deal with what crops up as honestly as we can.

Youngsters are picking up all sorts of sexual information from their friends and, if you don't reject that kind of sexual knowledge, it doesn't leave the individual feeling isolated with whatever worry they have. If, as adults, we are over-strict, that makes children either passive and spineless or totally rejecting and rebellious. Sloppy adult attitudes on the other hand, can drive young people into extremes of behaviour which they may not really want. So it *is* a tightrope — neither intrusive nor high-horse and distant. We clear everything with our parents. No question of keeping them out. Now and then we have an evening where we invite them to hear about our programme and they're quite happy — quite relieved in fact that we do it. And generally I feel that by acknowledging adolescent sexuality we at least stand a chance of bringing it within the realm of our guidance and support.'

Anne Jones had since left Vauxhall Manor, but the pro-gramme is still continuing under the present head, Gwen Evans. She said: 'We have altered the carrying out of the programme slightly, but in principle it is the same. We are pleased to be doing this work and consider it valuable for pupils and staff alike.'

Most schools however, leave all sex education in all its aspects to the biology teacher to cover in a lesson or two. Others call in health visitors, midwives or the local GP, others call in the FPA, and a few rely on the sales representatives of a tampon company which advertises itself as being available for talks in schools, at no charge. And this can be very tempting, for another cry which greets you in the staff room these days is: 'You cost so much.' On the surface, an insulting comment to make to people who do a morning's work for £10; but explained by school budgets. One teacher who told me I cost too much explained that his yearly budget in 1980–81 for general studies was £400, and that in the previous year we (the FPA) had taken up half of it. I could see his problem and I am pleased to say he could see ours. Working for £6 an hour seems a reasonable salary when you work that out on the basis of an eight-hour day, but days do not work out that way, for there is no payment for travelling time, or for time spent discussing problem pupils with the staff, or for time during break spent talking with the pupils themselves, or, indeed, for time spent preparing work.

But no amount of extra money would encourage some teachers to consider sex education because, intrinsically, the headmaster and sometimes the staff, too, think the subject should not be on the school curriculum. They believe that sexuality should not be brought through the school gates, or that if it is, it should be put in a cupboard until the children go home. They wish to avoid the idea that sexuality is within a child's experience, and should therefore be accommodated along with other experiences which make up his or her life. It seems an act of quite staggering obstinacy to be teaching pupils during puberty and at the same time to view sexuality as the one subject which is taboo. Not only do I think teachers who feel this way have not thought through the subject of sexuality; I also believe they have not thought through the subject of education either. They are trapped in the narrow, confining tunnel of schooling or training and have not the breadth of vision to see education for what it is, a living process. Yet if education is a living process and we are sexual beings, how do they defend such attitudes?

One of the best illustrations I can give of the absence of vision present at 'the top' is a meeting with an Education Minister who had heard that I was writing a book on education. He approached me to ask what my book was about and I began to reply: 'It's about sex education. . . .' and was about to go on when he said loudly, emphatically and with immense satisfaction: 'My views on sex education go back to the tenth century — BC.'

His obvious pride in this statement angered me, and I charged him with being a reactionary, to which he replied: 'If you call it reactionary not to want people like you interfering with my children then yes I am.'

I do not know why anyone should take pride in having a view which dates back to the tenth century BC, unless it illuminates a truth which has been obscured by time and the passing of civilizations. When that person is a Minister of Education I understand only too clearly why so many schools train and not educate. But I also understand why he would use a pejorative word like 'interfering' to describe the education we are involved in. The word 'interfering' is a highly charged one to use. Newspaper reports containing accounts of assault or murder cases used to include statements like: 'Police said the girl had been sexually *interfered* with.' So the use of the word is very serious. It alludes to the sexual assaulting of children, which is one of the gravest charges you can bring against an adult, particularly one who is a teacher. It is a politically and emotionally powerful word which I am sure has won him many votes.

'I gather you are here to discuss contraception,' said a teacher in a staff room. (She did not give me time to say that this was not the case.) 'You might as well know I have, with the full permission of the head, withdrawn my daughter from your class. I do not want her exposed to such things.'

At the same school, which I also visited for a number of years, there was an incident one year which caused a bit of a stir. I arrived one morning, after having also taught in the school the previous day, to be greeted by anxious faces in the staff room. There had been a complaint from one of the boys' fathers about my lesson. I asked what the complaint was and if they would like me to meet the father. The nature of the complaint wasn't known at that moment, but the father was coming in to discuss the matter. With that cloud over my head I went into another group. By the time I had finished the father had left the school.

'What did he have to say?' I asked.

'Oh, that his son had been sexually assaulted on his way home.'

'What happened?' I asked in alarm.

'A man tried to pick him up. He ran home.'

I waited.

'Why was he complaining about my session?' I asked.

'He wasn't,' the teacher replied. 'But the boy mentioned he had had some sex education during the day, and the father was concerned.'

'Is he still?'

'No,' the teacher said, 'He's quite happy for the boy to stay in your sessions.'

I thought that was the end of the matter. But the following year a staff member rang up our organizer to book us to come in, saying she only wanted two sessions instead of the customary four, and only wanted straightforward contraception, abortion and VD covered. She wanted only information, and none of the role-play and discussions which I always instigate.

When I rang this teacher, she referred to the father's visit the year before and said they had decided to tighten up on sex education.

'But he wasn't objecting to sex education,' I said.

'No, but you can never be too careful,' she replied.

I explained all this to our organizer and also refused to do the sessions. She knows I will not be a paid mechanic, especially where human feelings are involved.

Because of attitudes like these it seems to me vital that all schools take the time to organize a full discussion on sex education, for while they do not, the people who suffer are the pupils. I am thinking, particularly, of an occasion, in a south London comprehensive which concerned a friend who is a poet and novelist of some stature. She had been employed by the Arts Council on a writers-in-schools project where she went into secondary schools, and in this case, was asked to work with pupils to encourage their appreciation of poetry. She had agreed a programme with the headmaster, that she would be in school for four ninety-minute sessions during which pupils would be asked to write poems of their own with her help. These would afterwards be published in a magazine, which she would edit. She was to be responsible for the material in it.

She was working with 16-year-olds, some of whom were difficult, particularly one boy who was, initially, taciturn and unco-operative. She spent some time encouraging him to express whatever feelings were obviously ailing him, and he began, obliquely, talking about sex. She tried to give him confidence by saying that it was quite all right to write a poem about sex since much excellent poetry had been written on this subject. The following week she read them some poetry where sex was either implicitly or explicitly a dominant theme and the boy became more 'at home'. When all the poems were written she noticed that he had produced what she calls 'a banana poem' likening the penis to a banana. She only glanced at it before putting it in a folder along with all the other poems which she left, for the time being, at the school. In her words: 'It was not actually a crude poem, but rather a funny sad one.'

When she came to edit the poetry for the magazine, the 'banana' poem was missing. She saw the head about it. He said it was a disgusting poem and he had confiscated it. Furious, she reminded him that they had agreed that she was responsible for the material the pupils produced. He refused to allow her the poem. She argued that the pupil who had written it had been encouraged by her to speak about his innermost thoughts and that he would feel betrayed. She had tried to help him by saying that what he was feeling was acceptable and now he would feel doubly rejected since what he had produced had apparently been spurned. The head was unmoved. My friend was not. She was most concerned that a boy who already had difficulty in feeling accepted in the world should be dealt this kind of blow.

Pupils suffer in many ways through having their sexuality rejected, and this suffering begins when they are young. I do not teach in primary schools, but friends do, and have told me many stories, one of which concerns an eight-year-old boy, who was a 'star' pupil. My friend was therefore surprised to find him in a terrible state standing outside the headmistress's study.

'He was sobbing his heart out,' she said. 'I thought perhaps something had gone badly wrong at home, that his mother was ill or something, so I went to comfort him. But he wouldn't tell me what was wrong. It took me ages to get it out of him. All I could learn was that the headmistress had told him to stand outside her study after lunch every day for a week to show how naughty he was. The poor chap eventually whispered to me what he'd done wrong — "showing me diddle, Miss" — and I was horrified. Honestly, I nearly cried myself, I was so ashamed that an adult could be so callous. Here he was being publicly humiliated and disgraced in a way that he would never forget for the rest of his life. Obviously I went in to see the head, but she wouldn't budge. She said he had to be "taught a lesson". So I resigned. That was all I felt I could do. But I still think about that boy, even now, and the effects that experience must have had on him.'

I have come across other less extreme incidents which none-theless reflect attitudes about children's sexuality which should concern us. A deputy head of a school in Oxfordshire used to teach 5- and 6-year-olds. Some of the children played with themselves occasionally, something which Jan ignored, unless it became excessive, in which case she found them something different to do! She explained this by saying: 'I think the less fuss I make about it the better. If it is a phase they haven't been allowed to go through at home then they need to go through it at some time and better now than when they're sixteen or thirty!'

But Jan's actions — or lack of them — met with disapproval from a mother who came in to see her in a state of near fury. Her daughter (let us call her Cynthia) had told her that a boy had been exposing himself (the mother's words). The mother was very angry about this and wanted to know what sort of school Jan was running. Jan tried to explain this by saying that they were only children after all, but the mother would have none of it. If it happened again she would 'take the matter further'.

So Jan felt she had to comply with the mother's wishes, but without offending the boy. The next time the boy 'exposed' himself she therefore said: 'Put it away, Johnny, there's a good boy. Cynthia's mummy doesn't like it.'

Another incident involves a colleague who teaches sex education whose bringing up of her only son had obviously been too enlightened for his nursery school, for he came back after his first day with a huge smile on his face saying: 'I haven't got to go back tomorrow, mummy, I can stay at home.'

The following morning she took him in to find out what it was all about and it was, in essence, this, the teacher had been wearing long, stripey socks. My colleague's son had exclaimed: 'My mummy's got socks like that. They go all the way up to her 'gina [meaning "vagina"].'

For this offence he was sent packing and told not to come back until he stopped being so rude. Luckily the boy has such a sunny temperament that one of the most annoying aspects of his 'telling off' from the teacher's point of view must have been the fact that he could not be made to feel put out by it!

The public humiliation of children for being sexual people, or in other words, our inability to accommodate young people's sexuality helpfully, is a loss for all of us. We lose immediately in the loss of love, humour, compassion and friendship which are experienced through the process of helping others to a fuller realization of themselves, and we lose in the long term, when people who might have shown us good will, grow up estranged from us instead. The colloquial phrase for it is, 'The Generation Gap' and it happens when two or three are gathered together and one elects to be the top dog. Toppling the top dog then becomes a boring exercise which takes up much of the energy which could be used for more constructive purposes. The 'generation gap' bothers me a great deal. I spend a lot of time trying to bridge it. But it is unbridgeable while adults feel they have an inalienable right to their preferences and children do not have the same right to theirs.

I remember, particularly, a talk I gave to some people who had just qualified as trainee teachers and who were about to set out on their first teaching assignments. This talk was entitled: 'Fear and Affection in Education' and I described my conviction that it is impossible to educate without respect for children and affection for them.

The talk was well received, and I stayed for about an hour afterwards so that people could tackle me about it. One girl did. She said: 'I teach handicapped children, and while I accept the principle of what you say, it just doesn't work in practice. I know it doesn't.'

I asked her to explain how she knew this and what her experiences were. She said: 'I work with these kids; they're very exhausting to work with, and you have to draw a line somewhere, and I draw that line round being touched. It's all very well you talking about the rights of the child, what about the rights of the teacher? I have a right not to be touched, just as much as a child has a right to be touched'

I asked her whether she accepted that a child does have a right *to* be touched if he or she wanted to be. 'Yes,' she agreed, 'but I have my own needs, and I don't like being touched.'

'Then why are you teaching handicapped children?' I asked, and she replied plainly: 'Because I want to.'

I explained that during a month I had spent at a home for mentally and physically handicapped children one of the most evident needs of those children was to touch and be touched. I asked her if, considering this particular need on their part, whether she might not consider teaching in an area where this need was not so pressing.

She replied: 'You talk about needs, and my point is that I have needs too.'

'I agree with you completely,' I said, 'and it strikes me that one of your biggest needs may be *not* to teach handicapped children.'

That session took place in 1981. The people who were going out to be teachers, who all had degrees and a teacher training certificate, told me they had received no guidance on, let alone a full programme of sex education during the whole of the four years they had been training. Was this why a girl who had elected to teach handicapped children had not been able to discuss openly her hostility to being touched? Would anyone in their right senses allow a teacher to specialize in the care of the physically and mentally handicapped when that teacher had an aversion to being touched? Surely this is a tragedy for the teacher and her pupils.

And I understand all too clearly how that tragedy is perpetuated from generation to generation when I read documents like the official House of Lords report of 14 January 1976. This has been the last major debate on sex education for what is now nearly a decade. Questions about sex education come up from time to time, as when the question of DHSS funding to the FPA came up in the House of Commons discussion on 4 August

1980. In the discourse, which went on for just over an hour, Jill Knight, Conservative MP for Edgbaston and Chairman of the All Party Lords and Commons Family and Child Protection Group, argued that the FPA should not get funding from the DHSS to break the laws of the land by giving contraceptives to innocent children. As it happened, the FPA grant was slightly increased that year.

In the House of Lords debate sex education was discussed for seven hours. (Those wishing to read the full text will find them in Hansard Vol 367 No 18). Baroness Elles, at that time Chairman of the Conservative Party International Office and Opposition front bench spokesman, opened with a claim that it was time the House paid some attention to the matter of sex education in schools. She said among other things:

'Unlike the teaching of other subjects, such as history, geography or indeed mathematics, which are concerned primarily with the imparting of information and the extension of knowledge with the effect of developing the mind of the child, sex education can and does influence not only the mental understanding of a child but also has, or may have, an immediate and future impact on patterns of behaviour, social attitudes, emotional, psychological and physical experience. It affects a very personal area of a child's life, and the results of such education can be far reaching and lasting.

It can profoundly affect his or her physical and mental health as well as personal relationships both now and in adult life. . . .

What is sex education about? It does not deal only with sexual matters. . . . It also deals with moral education. It can have the effect of bringing up children to live according to the rules accepted by society as being reasonable and in the best interests of all within society, or it can be directed to changing the climate and mores of society. Therefore, the importance attached to this subject is considerable, equally in the manner in which it is taught, in who teaches it, in the aims and objectives of those who teach it, in where it is taught, in the effects of such teaching and in how far these effects can be measured, either scientifically or otherwise.

In drawing attention to the situation in regard to sex

education in schools, it must be said from the outset that it varies greatly both as between local education authorities and within local education authorities. It is well to recall that there is no statutory obligation on head teachers to provide sex education as such in the school, nor, if it is taught, for it to be confined to any particular course. The Education Act 1944 lays down the obligation on local education authorities to contribute towards the spiritual, moral, mental and physical development of the community by securing that efficient education throughout these stages — and that refers to the three stages within the school system — shall be available to meet the needs of the population of their area. . . .

In conclusion . . . I would just read these few recommendations. First, to withdraw from and withhold public subsidies to organizations concerned in the sale of contraceptives and engaged in commercial activities and the providing of abortions for profit in the private sector. Second, the right of parents to withdraw their child from any class on sex education without fear of reprisal either to the parent or to the child. Third, the maintenance and strong enforcement of the laws of the land, laws which are here to protect children, and, in particular, those laws which relate to the age of consent, to proper information to parents and to the family doctor and to the distribution of oral contraceptives. Fourth, the adequate control of films shown to children (wherever they may be) and shown with no censorship and with considerable licence. Fifth, the failure rate should be shown on non-medical contraceptives. If the Government can arrange to have warnings on packets of cigarettes which create a danger merely many years ahead, why should not a warning be put on contraceptives which in five minutes can cause tragedy to at least one if not two human beings? Above all, Government policies should take into account their responsibilities and should be concerted to support and not to divide the unity of the family and to take positive steps to protect the health and happiness of our children. . . .'

Another speaker, Lord Sudeley, made observations about 'moral degeneracy' and 'sexual promiscuity' which he went so far as to suspect 'was assisted by the sex education which is the subject of this debate'. It was, however, Lord Somers who summed up the extremist position for the anti-sex education lobby. Ill-informed and head-in-the-sand though his attitude was, this kind of thing I and my colleagues still find levelled at us. He said:

'The first point I want to raise is this. Is sex education, as it is generally supposed to be at the present time, really necessary, and if so, why? Of course it has been recognized for some time that an excessive birthrate leads to overpopulation, but we have heard from several noble Lords today that the birthrate has come down, so there seems to be no particular urgency about that. It seems to me that the only education that is necessary is, first of all, when to restrain from sexual intercourse, and, secondly, that fact that it must be confined to married couples, together with an understanding of the very grave danger of not so confining it.

My Lords, my noble friend Lady Loudon mentioned among other social evils, alcohol. What would we think of a Government Department (or, for that matter, an independent society) which was going round educating our young with propaganda that alcohol was a very desirable thing and that you gained a lot of pleasure from it, but giving no warning of the fact that it could lead to very disastrous things? I am not a teetotaller myself — at least certainly not a willing one — but there is no doubt that alcohol can lead to a very grave disaster unless it is used in moderation. It is exactly the same with sexual intercourse. If it is used properly it can be of great benefit and lead to great happiness: if it is used outside the marital relationship it can lead to disaster.

But the Family Planning Association are teaching the exact opposite. They are teaching our young people, many of them under 16, that sexual intercourse is a very desirable thing, giving great excitement and benefit, and that you have not really fulfilled yourself until you have experienced it. They divorce it entirely from the love motive, or from the marital status for that matter, neither of which two things seem to be of very much importance to them.

They also distribute all these contraceptives to the

young, but — and this is very important — they give no warning whatsoever to the young of the failure rate of these contraceptives, which in some cases is quite considerable. Nor do they warn young girls that the taking of the pill can lead to very undesirable effects. . . .

The ideal teachers are, of course, always the child's own parents. But one has got to recognize the fact that not all parents are as responsible as they might be and therefore we must make some provision for it. But I am very firm about one thing and that is that those parents who wish to do it themselves should have the right to withdraw their children from the instruction in schools.

We now come to the question of the kind of instruction that is necessary. I dare say that there are many who will think that my views are hopelessly outdated and old-fashioned. I do not agree with that. I do not think that Christianity is outdated. It is as new and vital today as it was when it first appeared on earth nearly two thousand years ago. I am convinced that this instruction should emphasise the virtue of Christian morality and should make it quite plain that a departure from this is not only morally wrong but physically dangerous. In fact, as I have already said, what young people need is the knowledge that sexual intercourse is not a thing to be played with. It is a thing to be taken very seriously. When it is properly used it can bring enormous joy and benefit to the family; but when it is abused it can be very dangerous and degenerating.

The difficulty about the selection of those who should teach it is that in the much larger schools of today the headmaster does not always find it very easy to know exactly what is going on in his school. Therefore I think we should be very careful indeed as to what qualifications are required for teaching this subject. Possibly the teacher should have a medical degree. I think that would be important and I, personally, should like him also to be a practising Christian. Many may decry such a view; but we are nominally still a Christian country and I feel, multi-racialism or no, that it is high time we became one again in fact. . . .'

Another complaint, voiced by Lord MacLeod of Fuinary, at one time Scottish chaplain to the Queen, was of the lack of reverence for and appreciation of the spiritual qualities of sex. This is true, but not the fault of sex education, but of consumerism and commercialization. This speaker also deplored the nuclear arms race. I, too, would like to say to the people whose financial investment is in the arms race 'take your bombs out of my heart', but I am sure they would not listen. People who teach sex education are told they cost too much; people who are making themselves fortunes from bringing us nearer to global catastrophe continue to amass wealth.

The quotations from this debate are still representative of the outdated attitudes towards sex education that I and my colleagues encounter nearly all the time. It is a subject in which there has been little enlightenment or progress.

I would like to see properly devised programmes of sex education set up in all schools, under the charge of people who care about educating the young, not mere teaching technicians. I would like to see schools setting aside more than one hour to cover sex education (all the time some schools allocate to us) and I would like to see sex educators themselves educated. I would like to see sex education initiated, not as a deterrent, a shock response to VD figures, but as a positive investment in the future, as an affirmation that we indeed want young people to grow up sound in mind and body. But for that to happen, policy makers are going to have to decide that sexuality is important, not because their hands are forced by the figures on illegitimate births, but because they understand that we cannot divorce our feelings from our intellect, and that it is attempts to do that which have resulted in acts of monstrous barbarism by clever men.

While there are headmistresses who have to disguise sex as hygiene, headmasters who do not want to recognize what is being taught in their schools, and while there are form teachers who do not bother to introduce you to the pupils, the subject is not being 'dealt with' but avoided. I think it is indeed time we had a *proper* debate.

10 Holistic Education

NOTHING IN my own teacher training prepared me for the rich and varied interaction I now experience when teaching sex education — nothing whatsoever. In common with many other students I was taught in what I can only describe as semi-meaningless jargon at the well-regarded institution in which I began my training. I did not complete that training because my plea that I was as unfamiliar with 'how to teach' when I left as when I arrived, fell on deaf ears. It was evading the issue to console me, as lecturers did, with my good marks because I believe then, and now know for certain, that they were gained within a vacuum; such was my ignorance of the fundamental and underlying principles of education. The bedrock of teaching was missing. Teaching was a mystery to me and there was no one on the college staff who would validate my fears or who was able to give me any positive help.

All this made me not want to teach at all. So I left teacher training college and turned to writing. I wrote some newspaper articles and was offered a reporting job on *The South Wales Echo* in Cardiff. Two years later, at twenty-one, I joined a national newspaper and my career in journalism began to gather pace. I did radio interviewing, television research, had my own column in Fleet Street, and eventually decided to freelance. Then, later, I returned to teaching.

During the course of writing an article about sexuality I interviewed a doctor who worked with the Family Planning Association (FPA). The interview went extremely well and she was pleased that I had asked 'interested' questions rather than loaded ones. When I told her at lunch afterwards I had once wanted to be a teacher and was still deeply interested in education, she suggested that I return to the educational fold. She explained that she taught sex education in schools and that there was an increasing demand for more people to do the work. In view of my earlier, although incomplete teacher training, she asked if I would be prepared to train with the FPA at my own expense to take on some of this work. I decided to attend a meeting to find out what it was about.

The meeting remains in my mind as one of the most significant I have ever attended because it was the beginning of a change in perception which has also altered the course of my career, and many other things in my life. It was called by the FPA to recruit people to train as sex educators to work in schools and youth clubs mainly, but also to work with adult groups interested in sexuality. Present at the meeting were about fifteen people, all of whom were women. They ranged considerably in age, ability and occupation. There were health visitors, nurses, social workers, mothers and myself. Some of us had degrees or professional qualifications, and some did not. We were all between the ages of twenty-five and sixty. The two women introducing the courses were FPA speakers who had been working both in schools and with adult groups for some years. One was in her mid-thirties and the other in her mid-fifties.

The first thing to strike me was what I can only describe as the 'gentleness' of the occasion; and I was disconcerted. I had expected something far more highpowered. As it was, the two group leaders introduced themselves fully, explaining who they were, how many years they had been with the FPA, what other work they did and what their backgrounds were. Then they asked us all, in turn, to do the same things. I secretly thought: 'Isn't all this a bit of a waste of time?'

I would like to stop there for a moment and explain that that meeting set the tone for all the meetings and sessions we were involved in and I now perceive it very differently from the way I did at the time. I see that the words used were 'speakers', 'educators', 'workshops', 'sessions'. I also see that the words current in the teacher training college I attended were: 'lecturers', 'training', 'tutorials', and 'structuring'. The difference is fundamental. One group of words implies involvement and co-operation and the other, a system of handing out information. Is it any wonder we still view education as instruction?

After the introductions we were told a little about what sex education entailed, that it included information on contraception, abortion, and VD but that, more importantly than this, it involved being able to be with young people in a comfortable, supportive and unaggressive way. They then asked each one of us why we were interested in doing this work, a key question in fact, which made me realize that at no time during the interview

I attended for entry into teacher training college at the age of eighteen was I asked the question: 'Why do you want to teach?'

The leaders included themselves in the question and when it was her turn, one of them said: 'I do the work because I am interested in sex.' The buzz which went round the room signified that her comment had found its mark. My own initial reaction was one of shock. These ladies had seemed gentle and 'proper' up till now. Was this a sign that they were not? Swift on that reaction followed the revelation of what it said about *me* — that I, too, basically viewed sex as something unwholesome and not quite 'right', for why else should I be shocked at someone openly declaring an interest in it? Why else were we there if we did not have an interest in the subject?

In a general discussion of our reactions — during which it became clear that that frank assertion, while true, was deliberately made — we realized how declaring an interest in sex leaves you open to attack. The comments of the noble lords in the previous chapter illustrate how easy it is to envisage the reaction many people would have to the statement: 'I am interested in sex': 'There, I told you so: they're all a bunch of sex maniacs. If we can't keep them quiet, then let's at least keep them away from our children.' Yet if you asked an English master: 'Why do you teach English?' he would say: 'Because I like the subject.' It is hardly abnormal to like, or to have an interest in your specialist subject, but if that subject is sex there is no doubt you will suffer discrimination. This makes nonsense of claims that we live in sexually liberated times. As one of our speakers once said at a meeting: 'It's taking sex seriously that gets you into trouble. If I was prepared to be flippant about it people wouldn't mind so much. *I could say I was a stripper more easily than I could say I'm a sex educator in some places I know.*' From my own experience there is a lot of truth in that.

After that meeting, those of us who were interested in continuing were asked to prepare a short talk on a choice of subjects for the next meeting. All of us wished to continue, and we all went away to prepare fifteen-minute talks. When we returned to give them, all of us discussed the content and presentation of each one, and what I did not realize at the time was that the group leaders were watching *all* of this. In other words how you 'were' with other people, how you became involved in spontaneous discussion was as important, if not more so, than how 'well' you delivered your prepared work. And those spontaneous discussions brought up many revealing attitudes among us. One woman, for example, exclaimed at one point: 'Of course I'm going to be worried about a homosexual teaching my son.' This was said after we had had a workshop on sexuality where it was demonstrated that homosexuality is a *part* of sexuality and not a deviation from it, and that it was very important in schools not to discriminate against the people in the class who might be homosexual. This woman realized what she had said, and blushed deeply, and a leader came to her rescue by saying that it was important that we find out what our real attitudes are. 'That is part of the reason for being here. Unless we find out about them, we can't deal with them. Many of us have repressed attitudes about homosexuality.'

Most of the education I took part in so as to become a sex educator was informal. Sometimes we had visiting speakers but even then, it was always in an informal setting. These speakers were doctors, people working with physically handicapped, a headmistress, a clinic nurse, a GP, and other people interested in human relationships. The bulk of the work we did together in the form of role-play and sessions where we all sat round and worked with each other under the guidance of a leader or as leaders ourselves. We were encouraged to talk, to express our feelings, to find ways of working with each other so that groups were self-regulating — that is, if one person 'hogged the floor' too much the others would let her know this without alienating her. All this I now see as being invaluable to my teaching in the classroom, or anywhere else.

We were led to explore our thoughts and feelings to see what they really were and we did this in a warm and supportive atmosphere, which we learned how to create, as well as enjoy, where none of us felt ridiculed for making a mistake or exposed for being honest. We were asked to challenge our attitudes, to find out why we had them and what they said about us, and to do this with other people in a way which enabled us all to explore without fear of meeting with a terrible accident. We were like mountaineers linked by ropes, each important to each other's success and safety. And from this I found, unwittingly to begin with, that I grew strong and skilful. I learned to enjoy the climb, to be responsive to tugs on the rope from other people, and to find companionship and harmony. It is not therefore surprising that I teach in the way I do. It is a reflection of the way I myself was educated.

At the end of this course we were asked to make a half-hour presentation to our peers in front of a panel of FPA officials and speakers, and to be involved in a day's session where everyone else did the same thing. On this it was worked out whether or not we should become sex educators. Most of us did, and a few did not. As a result of those sessions we became so close to each other that we formed a 'support group' which still continues, meeting seven or eight times a year to discuss work, to pool our resources, to help each other with particular problems related to our teaching, and to discuss our feelings generally. I look forward to attending the meetings for the friendship and humour they provide.

At a recent meeting one of the organizers recounted a funny incident. She had been informed from the clinics that a number of men were complaining about sheaths being too small for them. This was first of all put down to 'male fantasy'. But since the complaints kept on arriving she asked the manufacturers of the sheaths what they had to say about this. After all, women were running the risk of pregnancies. A meeting with the manufacturers took place in the FPA boardroom. To illustrate the point about sheaths being ample and flexible enough to meet demands, the manufacturers blew up half a dozen of them and they floated off, balloon-like towards the high ceiling. And there they stayed. Another meeting was due to take place and there was a panic about how to get them down. Someone eventually hit on a bright idea, and set off for the pub returning with a packet of darts. Our 'leader' felt a trifle foolish shooting darts at condoms — but they did the trick.

The answer to the problem of the malfunctioning sheaths was probably misapplication. Although packets of sheaths contain instructions, they are, like instructions for wiring up stereo systems or putting together fit-it-yourself wardrobes, seldom clear to the consumer. I was glad of one form teacher who asked me, while I was talking about sheaths, to demonstrate, by using my fingers as a makeshift penis, exactly how they are used. She said, in front of the class, that many boys didn't really know how to put one on properly. Who, after all, shows them? I now do this with every class, and it is interesting to note how attentive the boys are when this is happening. In the clinics, a lot of time is spent with women in explaining how contraceptives work, but there is probably still not enough time spent with men.

The FPA began its work in schools following requests from

teachers and heads for talks on contraception, VD and abortion; and the work evolved from there. In the 1950s and 1960s, heads, doctors and health visitors began approaching the FPA, through its work on contraception, for information and training in this kind of area. Initially, the FPA ran sessions for para-medics to update them on the contraceptive side of health care, and gradually more and more of this work was needed. As the schools themselves began to request more work, in response to the sophistication of pupils, the FPA began sending in its own visiting speakers, just for one session. In those early days a family planning nurse or a health visitor who had attended an FPA course would give the 'nuts and bolts' on contraception, VD and abortion.

As the work expanded, it led the FPA to set up a special education unit in the early 1970s, and it was through this unit that, for a while, the FPA trained sex educators as such. People like myself were trained for work in schools in sex education programmes rather than in information giving. Alongside this work, the FPA began organizing courses for teachers so that they themselves could learn to do the work. And, in the long term, it is hoped this is how the work will develop and continue. It was realized, soon after the courses for people like myself were set up, that it would be impossible for the FPA to supply, for all schools, enough people to do this work. So the emphasis was switched to working with existing teachers. In time, people like myself will move to working with groups of teachers, but, for the present, the demand from schools for 'outsiders' to do the work still exists and is, where possible, being met.

The question of who should do this work is often discussed at our group meeting. Whenever I, personally, have asked young people who they would prefer to do it they invariably reply: 'People like you.' The way things are at the moment they would prefer an outsider. However, my experience of schools where sex education is accommodated by the staff makes me feel that young people can be happy with the staff doing the teaching, so long as the staff themselves are happy with it.

Meetings cover very different areas, depending on individual and collective needs, or the prevailing political climate. Some-times we might spend the whole time discussing new material or books, watching new films to see if they are suitable for use in schools, or discussing issues which arise from our work. Essen-tially I see the meetings as an opportunity for continuing friendships and for learning, perhaps only from chance comments.

One such comment which took me a long way further in my thinking was when we were discussing the subject of attention. One person in the room said that a boy in her class, whom she described as an exhibitionist, 'was only out for attention'. We discussed how boys want more attention than girls, and the ways in which they contrive to get it. We also discussed what we might do about this. Should we have some groups as single sex only, and then mix the groups at a later stage? After we had spent some time with this, one person said quietly: 'But when you think about it, what else *is* there? Is there anything else we have to give each other besides attention.'

It is observations like that which have helped me to think further about what we do in the classroom — and elsewhere. There is a quality of attention which is missing from most of the exchanges I am involved in. People are abstracted, distracted or preoccupied: very seldom are they eager to 'engage'. I invite young people to give their attention by offering as high a quality of attention as I am able to. What I will not do is to demand that they 'pay attention'. I want them to give and receive, not pay.

One recurrent complaint which crops up in the meetings is the paucity of men in our group. There have never been more than two since I joined it and for long periods of time there have been none. And we have spent some time discussing why this is so, and trying to find ways of altering it. We believe it is due to the fact that more women than men stay at home and that more women than men work part-time and can therefore fit in occasional teaching during the day with other work. But it is also, we feel, due to the insidious continuance of the idea that feelings, relationships and personal aspects of life are 'women's work' and that men have other (and they mean by that, more important) interests and pursuits. While there are far more men who now take an interest in bringing up children there are still not enough who have the career circumstances or the wish to be involved in sex education with young people.

This is worrying from two points of view. It reflects badly on sex education itself and puts it into the realm of 'women's work' which still has far less status than men's work; and it also means that certain aspects of the work are not done as well as they could be. I mean by that that there are certain circumstances which require 'a man for the job'. One example of this is the group of boys mentioned in Chapter 5 whose prevailing interest was blue movies. What they needed was a man to show them that you do not have to be uncaring in order to demonstrate your manliness. A woman could not show them that, because they do not respect women, and because she does not know exactly what it is like to be a man. However, if a man had demonstrated to them — by being these things — that gentleness, tenderness and curiosity are indeed part of the male experience, he may have got somewhere with them. I achieved very little.

Some groups of boys on the contrary are more comfortable with me than they would be with a man; they are less worried about 'making a fool of themselves', of asking questions they fear may make them appear stupid. We have in the past done quite a bit of work at IT (Intermediate Treatment) Centres with groups of young people who are in trouble with the police, and for this work it needs, perhaps ideally, a man and a woman. People could then see at first hand that a man and a woman can relate to each other in co-operative, nonviolent ways. They could see that a man need not feel 'put down' if a woman contradicts him, and, more important than anything, they could see what it is like for two people to work with each other in a respectful way. As it is, I have been to some centres and known that whatever I was able to do would not be enough. We need male speakers. We need to be able to supply the right person for the right occasion and while there are no men in the group a certain type of boy, and girl, is being neglected.

Another topic which crops up regularly in our support sessions, is the subject of the amount of time schools allow us, and the fact that some schools want us to work for nothing. There are two arguments against the latter, the first is that we should not have to work for nothing (even if we could afford this) and that if we did we would be viewed as non-professional. As it is many people are under the misapprehension that we are selling contraceptives. We are sometimes confused with tampon manufacturers' lecturers who offer their services free. Some schools, to my mind, avoid their full responsibilities by taking up this offer. But even though money is a problem, it is not the only one. For most head teachers sex education is very low on a list of priorities, so that even when money is available it is spent on other things. On the other hand, schools who say they would like to invite us in for full programmes, claim they can only afford to have us in once or twice.

The implications of that are that schools expect you to be able to 'teach' sex education in two or three hours. And it is when you try and do this that there is a danger of sex education taking place in a clinical way, for how can you possibly fit in even a small part of the work I have mentioned in this book in a few hours? (There is too much of the 'emergency service' attitude in the way schools regard us.) So when we look for the reason why programmes of sex education are, generally, too clinical, why do we blame sex educators? I would like to spend at least half a dozen long sessions with every group I visit. It is the policy makers, budget advisers and the schools themselves who make sure this does not happen, not I.

What we are mainly agreed upon in the group is that, ideally, the subject should be accommodated by the staff themselves, but the staff need educating in order for this to happen. Many teachers and trainee teachers are not willing to take the subject (any more than I would agree to retrain to teach physics) and even those who are find themselves unprepared. You cannot learn to become a sex educator in a weekend course. It needs far more time than that. You have to understand your own sexuality in order to be involved in sex education, and that does not come about in a few days, or even in a few weeks. At present young people say they do not want the embarrassment of members of the staff who take them for English Literature, also discussing VD with them. If the division between sexuality and 'the rest of us' did not exist, that conflict would not exist. There is no good reason why one cannot discuss VD and English Literature. We have managed to organize schooling so that it does not happen.

What has been revelationary for me about being a sex education teacher is what it has shown me about the the way sex is viewed in a society which claims to be enlightened. If I am fortunate, my work is viewed with suspicion; if not, with open hostility. It is rare for anyone to adopt a positive attitude towards it. The general assumptions made about sex education are often conflicting, but they are, in essence these:

That the subject is non-academic, therefore not important;

That because the subject is non-academic, the people involved in it are not very intelligent and know nothing about education;

That people in our society know all about sex in any case
and those of us who try and 'teach' it are jumping on to a
fashionable bandwagon;

That sex is natural and should not be taught;

That sex is subversive;

That it should not be discussed in public;

That it certainly should not be discussed in public with
under-age children.

However, if you are going to segregate sex as something young
people may not be educated about then you are not educating at
all, but are, instead, involved in the impossible and destructive
process of trying to separate the inseparable. Teachers who
cannot accommodate adolescent sexuality are not educating the
whole person: they cannot be when they are failing to acknowledge an integral aspect of the individual. But since education is
about the whole picture, then it must be about the whole person
— it must be holistic. As sex education contains elements of
history, psychology, sociology, mathematics and chemistry, so
all those subjects contain elements of sexuality.

At the moment, the people who 'do' sex education in the
schools I visit are the doctors, nurses, social workers, and others
I have mentioned in this chapter. If in the future it is taught by
the school staff we shall have to find ways, perhaps in the teacher
training colleges, perhaps elsewhere, of educating the educators.

Essentially, sex education, as it is so dubiously called, requires
people with a holistic approach. To achieve this, one has to dig
deep into one's own consciousness to find ways of relating with
pupils which are non-aggressive, and which educate them into
an understanding of themselves and others. The principles
which motivate the work carried out by the FPA are clearly laid
out in FPA policy statements:

That sexuality is an inseparable part of every person and
should be accepted as one aspect of the total human experience and be treated with honesty and sensitivity;

That all individuals should be concerned with other
people as well as themselves. This concern should be
fundamental to all human relationships;

That individuals should be responsible for their actions.

But how could this happen within the existing school syllabus? It would seem appropriate to look at that now, since, more than at any other time in our history, it is crucial to provide education which is addressed to the individual. Unemployment, or enforced leisure, looks like becoming a permanent feature of the western world, and in this context an education programme which is concerned with enabling people to relate to each other, and to fulfil themselves in other than strictly work-functioning ways, would seem not only welcome, but essential.

11 The Future?

THE KIND of work in which I am involved with pupils is made possible by my affection for them, my respect for them and our appreciation of the relationship we have together. It is an exciting as well as a demanding way of working, and as in group work of many kinds there are considerable opportunities for learning. One of the main ways this learning is made possible is by using a non-hierarchical str cture rather than the formal idea of a 'lesson': my place with young people is among them rather than in front of them. To be discussing tenderness with your back to a blackboard and rows of bepupilled desks in front of you seems bizarre to me. Could this by why tenderness is not usually discussed?

This way of working in groups, which is commonly used by the FPA, has made it possible for young people to approach me with their problems after sessions have ended. I'm sure they would not have done so had the setting been a formal one. The difficulty is that, even with breaktime or lunchtime talks added on, the amount of time spent with each group is so limited. It is limited because of the very narrow idea that most people have of our roles as sex educators, and of our work. Originally the work literally involved what we call 'one-off' sessions. What the schools wanted was someone who would come in for an hour and explain contraception, abortion and VD. They wanted these subjects 'covered' from the information point of view and we had no brief, or time, to embark on anything else. Schools felt that the biology teacher did the reproductive aspect and that we were the logical sequence. And since we have no mandate to teach — we are invited in at the head teacher's discretion — we were not in a position to do much about this.

It has been interesting to see the variety of different headings we have been called in under during the years. I have been listed under domestic science, general studies, social studies, home economics, child care, general science, biology, health care and sixthform options. I have been given many titles from 'sex expert', which I am not, to 'doctor', which I am certainly not: although it is worth noting that some of the schools would have been happy to call me the latter. If a doctor deals with the subject it is respectable, but if a mere sex educator deals with it, it is not.

Initially, the FPA didn't query this position in schools because it was felt that some information was better than nothing at all. It wasn't until a few of us began talking that we realized we were caught in a trap. We were giving information about contraception because this is all we were asked to do, but resistance to our work was precisely because of this: because young people were learning about contraception as a subject in itself rather than as an aspect of relationship. So we began to press for more time. We began to be innovative in our approach to schools rather than responsive. When schools called up asking for the standard one-off we took it upon ourselves to educate staff as to why we wouldn't do this. And, in the main, this worked. I myself did no more than a few 'one-off' sessions, mainly because I was so bad at them: I had a knack of being led off into discussions about related topics and would end up not having 'done' contraception at all.

The extra time, however, was subject to school budgets and the problems of timetabling. The schools generally agreed to us being given three or four double sessions. To allow more would mean, so they tell us, a major planning exercise. It would require rebudgeting and alterations to the curriculum to accommodate us in more than an *ad hoc* way. In any case, for many people working in sex education this amount of time was sufficient. Only a few schools have a broad enough view of the subject of sexuality in particular and of relationship in general to feel that work of the kind that I encourage in the classroom is important. And I know there are many trained sex educators who would not feel skilled enough to undertake this kind of work. They are far more comfortable operating within well defined boundaries.

I think these boundaries are narrowly defined while the subject is called what it is: 'sex education'. The words 'sex' and 'education' in one phrase invite criticism from practically every quarter and, while adults continue to believe that education means instruction not enquiry, the problem with the title will continue. Like the headmistress who told a biology teacher when he asked if he could invite in someone to do sex education: 'I am not going to have abortion teaching and training for sexual intercourse going on in my school.' Quite right. I wouldn't have it going on in any school of mine either!

Not only does the phrase, 'sex education' carry with it the notion of teaching young people how to have sex, but it is also far too narrow a definition, certainly for the kind of work in which I am involved. Yet the search for an alternative title has eluded us, and it is an important search if the work is to continue and expand. We have considered phrases like 'Human Relationships', 'Human Development', 'Personal Development', or 'Education for Living', but none of these seems to have the right 'ring'. And here we come back to The Word Game. It has not occurred to me to ask the pupils what phrase they would like used. I have often asked them this obliquely by putting up the phrase, 'Sex Education' on the board and asking them what they think it means, or what kind of enquiry they would expect or want us to be involved in as a result of it. It may be useful in future to play this kind of Word Game at the end of our sessions together, and try to find out from young people what title would have most meaning for them.

The phrase was coined by the FPA as being the most suitable and clear title to use at the time, and in a fair world that might be the case. However, since in reality the title has always, in my experience, incurred disapproval, I think it needs changing, perhaps in order that people be allowed to understand the work properly rather than resist it because of its label. The narrow definition that people have of sex education is, of course, indicative of something far more worrying than complaints against people like me. There is the feeling that knowledge of their sexuality must be kept from young people, implying that both our own capacity for physical fulfillment with a partner (sex), and our own process of enquiry and discovery (education) are less than satisfactory.

This shows in our inability to find expression for, and therefore to pass onto our young, the subtleties, textures and range of words and emotions which they need in order to grow. I can't be the first person to have noticed that certain expressive words are now rarely used by *any* young people. They do not use the word 'joy', but then how often do we? When I use the word, their reaction is often that of suddenly recalling something long forgotten. They are pleased by this rediscovery. The words, 'beauty', 'caring' and 'tenderness' are absent from their vocabularies. They have substituted the words 'pleasure' and 'feeling good' for what I know to be 'joy'. Do we mean the same thing? Possibly we do, sometimes, but having a fuller range of words helps you to describe feelings better.

The problem here is one of the defining role of language, for as we use language, so it defines us. If young people do not know how to express joy then the feeling of joy is affected by this. Therefore, if young people are using increasingly sloppy and brutal language, does this mean that they are feeling uncared for and brutalized?

I think it does. I was recently with a group of girls who seemed to fit the stereotype of perverse young women. They were completely taciturn and during our first hour together they said practically nothing. So I asked them to write down for me by the following week what they would like to talk about, and also any questions that they had. When I returned to open their pieces of paper I felt shocked by what I read. The brutality of their language was quite difficult to take; with questions like: 'If you get fucked, but not all the spunk goes in you, can you get VD?' 'If you get fucked up the cunt, but not all the way, could you get pregnant?' 'If you gobble a boy off, can you get scabs round your mouth?' I found myself reading the questions out loud in a calm voice, and feeling assaulted by them as I did so. But I answered them all with no hint of censure. I wasn't sure whether the girls had written in this way to try me out, or because this was the only language they had. And the following week I discovered it was a bit of both.

I went back, feeling apprehensive, for I knew I had to tackle this question of the unpleasantness of their language, but in case it was the only language they had I wanted to do this without offending them. And as so often happens, they did the work for me. There was a perceptible change of mood from the previous week. The girls were glad to see me and showed their friendliness and eagerness to begin the session.

One of the first things they let me know was that they had stopped being ashamed. I discovered, as they began to unfold, that they *were* ashamed of their language, but at the same time completely alienated from the only other language they had heard used for sex: the quasi-medical jargon of the human reproductive parts talked about in biology lessons. They had not been close to people who talked about sexuality in tender terms, so it had become, for them, the smutty business it has been for many human beings generation after generation. And yes, their flinging of their language at me was, in a sense, a deliberate onslaught. They were literally throwing their mess and conflict at me in much the same way that small children physically hurl themselves at you. And although they couldn't articulate this either, it had been a tremendous relief to them to have me not only withstand them, but look and behave as if I still liked them. It might mean they could trust me, as they did that third session. They let me know how difficult it was for them to talk about sex because they didn't know what words to use, and they also let me know, by their touching responses to my use of words like 'tenderness' that they yearned to be able to express themselves in other than brutal ways.

It is this that I have found so pronounced in the vast majority of the hundreds of young people I meet each year — a progressively more obvious inability to portray the kinds of qualities which are vital to their well-being and ours. What perturbs me is that the qualities — consideration, compassion, affection — are often there, but with practically no channel for young people to put them into effect in their own lives. As we saw in the 'non-battering families' session, this means the expression of joyful emotions is made less of a possibility.

It occurs to me that all this may be the reason for the resurgence in romantic fiction. Girls do bring this kind of material into school sometimes and I am beginning to understand why. It must be so inviting to turn to the stuff of 'happy ever after land' as an antidote to and substitute for harsh language and unexpressed desires.

These girls gave me a clear example of how language confines and defines. They were prisoners of their words, which were as injurious as blunt instruments in dulling their ability to experience what their words could not describe. And this process is circular, for if tenderness is imprisoned by language, so brutality is encouraged by it. It is my observation that the language young people use to describe feelings and sexuality is, in the main, unpleasant, even to them.

Sex education needs not only to be called something different, it needs to *be* different, for when I have examined from term to term what I do and what the likely results of the work may be, I am not at all satisfied. I am not satisfied because I feel the work needs to be contextualized and broadened into a recognizable form, so that other teachers can be fully involved. I have been told, for instance, that the way I teach is personal to me and therefore only available to me, and this is not the case. Since, in the FPA, we have now moved emphasis from recruiting sex educators to finding people who will instead be tutors working with adult groups, including teachers, in the field of sexuality and human relationships, it is time to look at what schools might be doing to take advantage of this. The FPA now runs courses especially for teachers who want to work in this area of 'relationship', and if schools considered sexuality an important enough area of enquiry they could be arranging for numbers of staff members to attend such courses.

As a result of these courses I have had to consider what I would like to see for the future of what we now call sex education and come to some conclusions about how to implement such work. In essence I believe there should be a full programme of 'relationship' operating in all secondary schools. The work should begin as soon as pupils enter the school, for it is ridiculous to wait until they are fourteen or fifteen.

It would of course, be important to train staff to do this kind of work. Some existing staff would feel comfortable with it after a small amount of training. This is the way I became involved. Others, and especially new teachers coming up through the colleges offer students courses in the subject of 'Relationship', perhaps in consultation with bodies who have already done work on this subject. At the moment the people who 'do' sex education in the schools I visit are doctors, nurses, social workers, health visitors and people like myself. In the future the whole concept of this work needs to be rethought and brought into a broad field of enquiry. We need to look at the whole area of human relationship: personal relations, professional into a broad field of enquiry. We need to look at the whole area of human relationship; personal relations, professional relations, social, economic and political relationships, and an individual's relationship with him or herself. The underlying purpose would be to educate young people to the idea of responsibility for themselves and others and to give them a broad enough appreciation of the way they fit into and relate to the world for them to act in significant and meaningful ways.

Before this can happen, parents, teachers and policy makers need to be convinced that a programme of Relationship is important. My own feeling is that the work is of paramount importance, especially in an economic climate where the combined effects of recession and technological development look like making full employment a thing of the past. But even with full employment it would seem vital to me that young people do not grow up in isolation, hopping around from compartment to compartment without ever discussing the links and inter-relationships which make up their lives. At the moment many schools teach in a way where cognitive learning is separated from feeling, when fundamentally these are inseparable, and where sexuality is put into a box marked 'adults only'. Segregation is the order of the day, and alienation the result of this. I see young people who cannot express themselves and who have no idea what it is like to feel related, in any other than a belligerent sense, to their surroundings.

In a world as complex as ours it is even more necessary that young people have the means of expressing their feelings and thoughts and of relating these to themselves and others. This way they may enter into relationships which sustain them and which in turn sustain others. At the moment fulfilling relationships are lost to thousands of young people through lack of example and through their failure to express themselves. Rather than shying away from our responsibilities to educate as fully as possible — to educate for life and living — I think we should be moving firmly and rapidly towards them.

Until we do this young people are being sold dreadfully short, and for that we all pay. We pay a heavy price for putting our futures in the hands of uneducated people who will know only how to perpetuate the mistakes passed on to them. If the teacher has tunnel vision, how is the pupil to learn? It is ostrich-like to invest in education and not in human feelings. The ostrich position is tragic for both adult and child. It leaves adults without consolation and children to fend for themselves.

Afterword

Since this book was completed Mrs Victoria Gillick won, and then finally lost, her campaign to make it illegal for under 16's to receive advice and treatment about sexuality without parental consent. While people generally may have believed that this related mainly to contraception, in fact schools were frightened enough to take Mrs Gillick's initial victory as meaning that teachers like myself could no longer work with under 16's. During the time when Mrs Gillick's campaign stood firm, between December 1984 and October 1985, I was not invited into schools to work with any pupils other than sixth-formers. For almost a year the schools who usually employed me — now as a freelance teacher — stopped doing so. In my own personal experience, therefore, many hundreds of 14- and 15-year-olds did not receive the kind of attention this book describes.

While sex education is not a properly formulated subject within school curriculi, it is not a proper subject and as such is prey to anyone's individual campaign to have it halted. Unless policy-makers and curriculi developers choose to accept the subject as important, it will continue as it is — a sporadic endeavour undertaken without commitment — and therefore indefensible when attacked. Part of my purpose in writing this book was to move sex education from this untenable position into an area of debate where it could be properly argued and constituted. For unless it is so, it will be prone to disappear whenever the going gets rough, and in particular will be vulnerable to any individual parent bringing an action against a school or teacher in respect of it. Ironically, while painful for the individuals involved, this may be what is needed to have a fair public debate on the subject.

I do not know the full reasons why Mrs Gillick's campaign was defeated and cannot therefore assess whether educational principles as described in this book were taken into account in reaching a decision. It was by a narrow margin — three votes to two — that the Law Lords, in October 1985, allowed an appeal by the DHSS against the Court of Appeal judgement won by Mrs Gillick in December 1984. While I and many others are grateful to all those involved in bringing about the House of Lords judgement, there is a lot more to be done.